MONTESS

MEMORY
ACTIVITY BOOK
FOR SENIORS

VERIFIED SOLUTIONS TO STRENGTHEN YOUR BRAIN
QUICKLY AND EASILY. ALSO USEFUL FOR ALZHEIMER'S,
POST-HEART ATTACK, AND DEMENTIA.

MICHEL BRAIN

TABLE OF CONTENTS

INTRODUCTION

The Montessori Method of teaching was invented in the year 1907 by Dr. Maria Montessori, and she began advocating it in the year 1914. In her pursuit of higher education in the field of educational history, psychology and philosophy, she came across every delightful nature of seniors. According to her, seniors like to work in a similar way as they like to play and therefore, she felt that seniors must be allowed to manifest their own educational thoughts and desires. They must be compelled to assert the social conventions of modern or post-modern era teaching. Instead, there should be a self-indulged liberating feature prevalent in their minds, regarding education, so that they can ace the primaries of life. Once they are self-independent at a primary stage, they will, later, be given more share of creativity that can navigate them through stress in a passionate way. Therefore, the Montessori Method focuses on seniors' mental cognition, and the following are the sets of principles and tactics that come in the ambit of this method.

You do not have to spend a ton of money to buy materials. They come in three categories: practical life, sensorial, and academic. Sensorial materials help seniors learn through their senses. Studies show that sensory learning plays a vital role in brain development. Sensorial information is useful in building neurological connections that are vital for reasoning. Montessori provides sensorial materials that are active and help seniors to connect with their senses. Montessori sensorial materials include "pink tower" and solid wood cubes in different sizes to promote visual understanding of dimensions. These materials can be expensive because they are long-lasting and can be used by men.

The method came about when Dr. Montessori discovered many problems with the standard traditional teaching methods. She noticed that the traditional system was fighting nature, instead of nurturing the potential. The method was designed so that seniors develop their skills on their own terms. It allows them the freedom to discover who they are, be who they are, and decide who they can be.

This book will explore various activities of Montessori, explain what the Montessori Method is, and what makes an activity a Montessori. There are many activities that seniors engage in, but not all of them are beneficial. Moreover, some activities do more harm than good because they do not foster important tenets of Montessori. This book will also look at the Montessori environment and what can be done to make it suitable for a senior. Maria Montessori emphasized the importance of preparing the environment and its role in learning. She established that seniors are not productive in a messy environment and advised teachers and seniors to provide a conducive environment for learning. This book explores the Montessori Method in detail and explains to seniors why they should use it.

CHAPTER 1
INTRODUCTION TO MONTESSORI METHOD

The Montessori approach encourages educators to "follow the senior." This is an excellent approach as it recognizes the evolutionary characteristics and needs of each senior at each age. Through this approach, educators build an environment for the seniors that's both spiritually and physically able to meet their needs. Because of this, their progress and development emerge as a need to adapt to their environment. Each senior has a need to give meaning to the world around them. Then they construct themselves in relation to their world.

The materials you would find inside a Montessori home each have a purpose as well. These materials are scientifically designed to pay special attention to the interests of seniors based on the developmental stages they are at when they enter the classroom. They are also created with the belief that when seniors are able to manipulate concrete objects, this helps develop their abstract thinking and their knowledge. The Montessori materials give seniors a chance to explore and investigate in an independent and personal way. They promote concentration and allow seniors to master concepts and skills through repetition.

No Montessori home is complete without an adult who is usually an educator, such as a directress. Each directress observes the seniors individually taking note of their interests, capabilities, and needs. Then they offer the senior opportunities to perform activities and use the materials with a specific and concrete purpose in mind. As seniors learn to work with purpose and in an intelligent manner, they also learn how to care for themselves and for their small community which, in this case, is the classroom.

The Montessori approach also allows seniors to explore different areas of understanding. From the time they start their Montessori journey, seniors are introduced to these areas that we will be discussing in detail later. These areas of learning focus on teaching seniors different concepts and helping them develop different skills. Since they have the freedom to explore these areas and work on the materials and activities found within them, they don't feel pressured to learn as fast as everyone else.

As a senior, learning all about the Montessori approach and everything it entails allows you to create your own prepared environment at home. You also learn the kind of materials and activities you can prepare for your senior to follow the Montessori approach at home. This provides them with consistency that, in turn, helps them learn more profoundly.

Fences, Not Mazes: The Abstract and Philosophy

This is the philosophy in which structure is created so that seniors can get their educational needs met whilst simultaneously feeling free. Connected to this are liberty and its subsequent balance with discipline. Liberty and discipline don't have to be counter to each other; they are two sides of the same coin, both necessary for learning and development.

Discipline is defined in a different way to mainstream education. In many homes, discipline is a type of punishment, a tool used to give seniors detention, limitation, or some sort of "telling off," as if they have done something wrong. Yet in Montessori discipline is seen and treated as a positive thing, a form of self-discipline to enhance learning. This is the fundamental difference between discipline in homes and normal educational frameworks and the self-discipline you find in the Montessori approach; the latter focuses on positivity and reward.

Your senior's environment is also an integral part of the philosophy's success. "Fences, not mazes" suggests that you as the use senior provide fence-sufficient borders or boundaries for safety and protection, not mazes. A maze, as you are aware, is a puzzle or a structure one may become lost in by taking many wrong turns. A fence provides a boundary and framework to keep one enclosed in. This philosophy still allows for the freedom of choice aspect to Montessori education—your senior is still allowed to possess creative, artistic, and academic freedom as it is primarily their own learning journey; however, there is a priority of boundaries or structures to work within, over endless choices or mazes that can take them down a wrong route.

Other important aspects to Montessori's philosophy that we have covered in other sections are the following:

- Freedom of choice
- Learning through practical life activities and skills
- The senior acting as a guide
- The importance of order
- Nature, community, and culture
- Development stages and sensitive periods
- Processes, not results
- "Help me to do it myself"

Open Systems and Approaches to Learning

This approach is contrary to the status quo. It requires much more preparation ahead of time and gentle guidance as the process unfolds. The open and prepared environment is an integral part of the systems and approaches to learning. In a prepared and open environment, activities are laid out; there are some forms of coding, such as color, shapes, or numbers, and the objects, furniture, and materials in the environment are shaped to the senior's needs. The environment is created to be "open"—a place where seniors feel free to move and walk around and choose each activity as they wish. In traditional Montessori classrooms, there are only senior-sized tables and chairs present.

It may be interesting to know that Dr. Montessori had her own furniture created when she was in search of senior-sized furniture for her classrooms and there were none to be found. Fortunately, this is not the case now, and you can find a senior-sized version for anything you wish to provide for your seniors within a Montessori framework. There is an abundance of materials and activities to make your open system and approach to learning as creative and limitless as possible. It is important to prepare your senior environment, so they have the foundations, educational materials, and setup necessary for development. Anything "closed," such as in mainstream or traditional classrooms, may seriously impact your senior's learning and put a limit on to how much freedom and choice they have.

The key to remember is that the open environment is based on your senior's development. It is designed to offer activities that match the sensitive periods and development stages, offering a wide interest of variety and skill introduction to your senior. Due to the openness and element of choice, every activity may not be used because providing an open system gives your seniors the opportunity to choose what may or may not resonate. In an open learning environment, it is also significant to shape structure around the different types of activities presented. For example, you may choose to order activities into the areas of practical life, sensory, math, and language. You may also have a unique area or section on culture or one exclusive to water or food-related activities. This complies with the sense of order necessary for your senior to thrive, yet within the open system framework.

Providing Purposeful Activities

Caregivers who have the chance to observe a Montessori home would see how quiet or calm it is. Often, these seniors wonder how they can make their own senior be the same way, at home. In the Montessori classroom, seniors work independently, move around the home carefully, and speak softly. Most, if not all seniors in the Montessori environment, do this because they are performing purposeful work.

By design, Montessori lessons provide seniors with purposeful or meaningful activities aligned with their needs at their current developmental stages. Much like adults, seniors can reach a state where they are calm and highly focused as long as they are able to find purposeful work where they can direct their energy.

Apart from giving them confidence and a sense of accomplishment, providing purposeful work to seniors is an excellent method to redirect undesirable behaviors. No matter how much energy a senior has (and there are A LOT of seniors who seem to have boundless energy) when they're given work that they find interesting and meaningful, they will be able to calm down, focus, and start their learning journey.

In "traditional classrooms," teachers often find it extremely challenging to redirect misbehaviors because all they do is remind the seniors of the rules, give them work in which they aren't interested, or try to negotiate by offering them rewards. Although some of these methods may work with some seniors, these aren't long-term solutions. Instead, they should take a few tips from the Montessori Method and provide these "misbehaving" seniors with tasks they enjoy, thus giving them a purpose.

For instance, if a senior is interested in animals, the teacher works with this interest. In the language area, the teacher can give the senior the large moveable alphabet, or LMA, along with animal pictures or objects. Then they can present the activity where the senior would match the animals with their beginning sounds that they can take from the LMA. In the cultural area, the seniors will find a lot of activities about animals. Any of these can serve as purposeful work for them. It's all about being creative in terms of providing activities to them that they will find interesting and meaningful.

While Maria Montessori worked, she observed how happy seniors were when performing purposeful work, especially when they have chosen the work themselves. In this way, seniors see their work more as play, but with a purpose. Of course, this doesn't mean that when seniors start breaking the rules, the teachers just watch them They must also be guided so that they know what's right and what's wrong. Remember, seniors may enjoy as much freedom as they need if they're not causing harm to themselves, their environment, or to others. When they all follow the rules of the classroom, they will be able to focus on the meaningful work they have chosen from the environment.

However, when you try forcing an activity on seniors, they won't find this meaningful. Seniors know what they need, and once they find it, the work becomes purposeful for them.

Adult Supervision: Guidance, Not Absolute Authority

This brings us to adult supervision and guidance. The best way to see yourself in your senior's learning journey is as the director or directress. You are merely a guide, providing the correct structures and frameworks and making sure you are a gentle force in your senior's educational life. The whole purpose of Montessori is for them to have the liberty to learn and to express themselves. There needs to be a sense of freedom for them to move around the room or home space you have created, and this can best be done when you are taking on a guiding and observing role.

As a director or directress, you are directing your senior's energy without controlling it. Control can have a negative and destructive effect on their natural and developmental urges and instincts, such as imposing a false sense of superiority or authority when it comes to their learning choices. Each senior is different, and between the ages of 65 to 100 you still can't truly know where your senior thrives. If you have a recomposed idea as to where you want your senior to excel, this could take away from their true path and their own needs and desires. You may be a buff, for example, and have little personal interest in art, practical life skills, or cooking. You may be highly musical and see your own kin as having a musical path ahead too, yet they may be inherently drawn to something highly academic, like math.

The key is to allow them freedom by observing their choices and gently guiding their way. You can offer input and suggestions, directing them towards activities they may have been neglecting; however, you should never force them into anything, especially if this force or "telling" results in any form of distress, tantrum, or extreme display of negative emotion. This would clearly be telling you the activity is out of alignment and in disharmony to their natural interests at the time. Remember, Montessori is a journey, and your senior has many years to experiment with all the activities presented. The best thing you can do, as the guide, is to have patience and redirect their energy when you best see fit.

If you are ever in doubt, the best thing to do is to look to Montessori's opposite. Traditional schooling has many positive points; of course, but the fundamental difference is in the approach to the role of the adult. Many seniors grow to develop resentments and feelings of restriction or limitation through their educational experiences. Sometimes, an imposed sense of authority can inhibit the learning process, and the teacher may come to be seen as the tyrant or authoritarian figure no senior resonates with. Observing these patterns may be able to assist you in shifting any blocks or limiting fears as to the role you play in your senior's journey, looking at what you don't want to be or embody to help you become who you do want to be.

Simultaneously, you can seek inspiration from the positive aspects of traditional and mainstream schooling. The authority element to teaching is useful when used in balance and moderation, and when used as a tool solely to help your senior's development.

This passage by Dr. Maria Montessori in *The Senior in the Family* portrays these notions accurately:

Ways to Supervise Your Senior While They Perform Montessori Activities

Although seniors get the most authentic experience of the Montessori Method in an actual Montessori environment, this doesn't mean that you can't apply the Montessori at home. Using similar activities and materials you can reinforce your senior's learning, even in the comfort of your own home.

Of course, you must remember your role as the adult in the Montessori environment. As much as possible, you must refrain from telling your senior what to do. Keep in mind that the Montessori approach encourages independence and freedom. Therefore, the role you will play in your Montessori setup is the same role played by Montessori teachers and directresses.

You should observe your seniors and merely supervise them as needed. Facilitate your senior's learning instead of directing it. In doing this, you will be able to successfully reinforce the Montessori Method in your home. To help you out, here are some ways you can supervise your seniors as they perform Montessori activities at home:

1. Allow your senior to perform practical life activities in the form of daily tasks and chores

When you learn more about the practical life area of the Montessori classroom, it's all about learning how to do real-life skills. Only in the Montessori classroom, everything is senior-sized. The sinks, tables, and chairs are lower, the sharp utensils have dull blades and points, the washcloths are smaller, the brooms and mops are smaller, and so on. All of these are part of the Montessori materials that have been specially designed and are part of the prepared environment.

Of course, you don't have to purchase all these special items for your senior just so they can use them at home, especially if you're on a budget. Instead, you can just show your senior how to use the real materials in your home to perform daily chores such as sweeping, washing dishes, cutting soft fruits and other soft food items using a dull knife, and more.

If your senior shows interest in a chore you normally do, you can present how it's done the right way. Start by showing your senior how to take the material, how to use it, and how to put it back when he's done. From there, observe whether your senior was able to follow everything you've taught them to find a different way to use the material. Seniors absolutely love doing the same things their seniors do. So, as long as the chore or activity is safe for your senior, show them how to do it!

2. Instill a love for language in your senior

In the language area, there are so many different things you can do with your senior. Although learning the alphabet is a huge part of any language, there are other activities you can do as well. Of course, you can also come up with your own materials like the ones in the Montessori classroom. For instance, you can easily recreate object drawers or object boxes. Simply place small objects that have the same beginning sound in small boxes or drawers. Then print out cards with the alphabets on them, laminate the cards, and stick them on the boxes or drawers. Then you can introduce them to your senior and make them part of your materials.

If they want to play with these materials, let them. Try to observe how they work with them. Do they sort the objects according to their beginning sounds or do they do something else? If they come to you and tell you a story about the objects in the box, listen with a smile and make eye contact as they are talking to you.

3. Provide your senior with manipulative

The best way to provide materials and concepts to your senior at home is by providing concrete materials or manipulative. Seniors absolutely love these materials because they're able to do so much with them. Again, if you prepared or created a material based on the real

Montessori materials, learn the method of teaching it too.

Then, when your senior shows interest in the material, present it to them, step back, and see how they work with it. If they don't damage the material or are not in danger of harming themselves, give your senior the freedom to work with the material as they see fit. Then when they ask you how to use it correctly, present the proper method once again.

4. Allow your senior to explore freely and discover things on their own

These are crucial to the Montessori Method. If you plan to create a Montessori environment in your home, you must familiarize yourself with the approach as well. Since you're reading this book, it means that you're really interested in learning all about Montessori and how you can apply it to your own senior, so that's a great start!

After learning about Montessori, you must also practice restraint when it comes to supervising your senior. Always remember that Montessori encourages independence. Therefore, when it's Montessori time at home, you must also assimilate the roles of a teacher, which are to observe, supervise, facilitate, and make sure to take care of your senior and that they don't damage the materials in the prepared environment.

Possibly, the most challenging thing you would have to face is to restrain yourself from stepping in. As a teacher, you always want to teach your senior the right way to do things. There's nothing wrong with this, of course. But if you really want to practice the Montessori Method, you must also practice. Supervision gives them the freedom to do their own thing and have fun while learning. So, when they step back into the Montessori classroom, they don't have to adjust to how things are done there. When you do the same things as the teachers in the Montessori classroom, you're providing your senior with the consistency they need to continue their Montessori learning.

CHAPTER 2
PRINCIPLES OF THE MONTESSORI PHILOSOPHY

The in-depth knowledge of the method, and the careful documentation made on the texts of Maria Montessori, allowed me to draw up a list of basic principles that I am drawing inspiration from. And I liked the idea of sharing it with you, adding my personal reflection to each "rule."

Use Positive Discipline

Montessori teaches us that every senior has come into the world with a special task to accomplish, and invites us to help them find their way by accentuating the positive side of things: using affirmative rather than negative forms, shifting the senior's attention rather than fighting frontally their will, praising positive actions and attitudes, and correcting negative ones.

No physical punishment, no shouting, threats and blackmail, no phrases such as "you are ugly," "you are bad" —seniors need a few clear rules, which must be explained calmly and patiently. They do not come into the world to make us angry; it is certainly not their intention to spite us. If they do it is only to communicate a malaise or a need that they cannot convey with words.

Give Them the Opportunity to Try New Experiences

How can we help a senior deal with what they would like to do on their own? Only by letting them try! I think this is one of the most difficult tests for us: letting our seniors do things that we would naturally do or forbidding them because we don't think they are up to par/ big enough, or because they are too dangerous.

I am convinced that seniors, even a few months old, are already able to self-regulate and recognize situations potentially at risk only if they are left free to deal with them. I would like to point out that this does not mean leaving your senior in disarray, simply involve them and make them participate in daily activities, such as setting and bringing dishes and glasses to the table or teaching them to climb the stairs, thus demonstrating to have faith in their abilities.

Don't Interrupt Their Moments of Concentration

The ability to concentrate is part of intelligence, and the senior must learn it over time. However, if every time they try to concentrate, they get distracted by your words, not only will they fail to learn, but they will end up believing that focusing is not important. What we see as a simple game for a senior is actually a very demanding activity. A real job. Therefore, in addition to not "making it easier" for them, doing it for them, we don't even have to interrupt it while they are concentrating on completing it.

Encourage Instead of Reward

In the Montessori homes, there are neither marks nor verifications. The senior does not need to be pigeonholed or to work for recognition. Their satisfaction comes from themselves. Instead of "that's so good," "what a treasure," give satisfaction to your senior with a compliment aimed at the success of the task or the positive attitude they have shown; tell them "what a beautiful circle you drew," "that kind that you have been."

Being a senior is not an easy task, I am realizing it with every passing day. Having a space for discussion and a place to vent doubts and fears is essential. The problem is that we are, but we don't realize it (also because nobody ever tells us that). The teachings of Maria Montessori can help us to raise independent and generous seniors and to draw our satisfaction from them.

Offer Them Choices

Let your senior have the possibility to choose in the little things that concern them: which fruit or which yogurt to eat, whether to wear a dress over another and so on. This will get them used to the difficult task of making a decision and make them feel part of the choices to be made.

The path to a senior's autonomy is long and dangerous. All the teachings of Maria Montessori are aimed at empowering them; respecting them in their choices and activities. Leaving them free to decide whether to put on the orange or yellow jersey is also a small step towards growth and maturity. Do not worry if the color combinations of their clothes are not the best, seniors are funny just when they are left free to dress as they like.

Limit the Number of Games Available

Choose games that are well made, educational, and beautiful. [...] Give the senior only one game at a time, and when they are older, teach them to tidy up each activity before starting another one.

Always Tell Them the Truth

A senior is able to understand much more than we expect. Explain things to them in simple words but always tell them the truth; don't make up stories that seem easier for you to understand in order to explain things to them. Don't even promise them what you can't keep. Here, I think broken promises are one of the worst things you can do to a senior. Never promise what you are not sure you can keep.

Forget the Clock

Try to understand when they are hungry and when they are sleepy. Try to offer them what they need when they need it and not when your organization says so. Enjoy every moment spent with your senior. Every minute is precious; a gift that must be fully enjoyed. I know at first it will seem difficult (and perhaps heavy) to give up your habits, but over time you will appreciate these little moments of joy more and more because they will be less and less. The senior will grow away from you a little, preferring to play with friends rather than being on the mat with you. And rightly so. So, take advantage of it now. When you are with your family, put away your watch (and smartphone!). The first memories of a senior will certainly not be the clean house, the friends who have come to visit you, or the thousands of games scattered around them. It will be the time spent with you.

Turn off the TV

It has been shown that for every hour spent in front of the TV before the age of two, your senior will have a 0% higher chance of having language and learning disorders. Background TV is also harmful, as it decreases the senior's ability to concentrate.

Since the princess arrived, the TV is always off here. We no longer watch the news, TV series, or movies in the evening. It has almost become an ornament. Sometimes, we miss it, but we have made a choice based on our daughter and we carry it forward with pride. When we are at the table, we fill the silences with songs for her, who is sitting there with us and looking for attention. In the evening we read a story, we roll on the carpet, and we are not afraid to invent absurd rhymes to keep her company and make her laugh.

Why Montessori

Seniors Enjoy Learning

In traditional homes, seniors don't have much choice; they are assigned work and expected to do it. When you tell a young senior to do something, it's like their instincts tell them to do the opposite. In Montessori, the seniors have the freedom to choose. They can follow their natural instincts and engage in activities of their own free will. When a senior decides to partake in an activity, it is because it has piqued their interest. The best thing about Montessori is that the seniors have fun and enjoy themselves while learning essential skills.

Montessori Promotes Independence

They have access to eye-level shelves that hold skill-developing materials. The senior can use real-life items that accommodate their height and size. They can partake in real-life activities such as cleaning, food preparation, caring for plants, among many others. Their environment presents all items that a senior would usually ask for, allowing them to engage with and complete tasks independently. Seniors feel a sense of satisfaction and pride when they do not have to ask for help and manage to find solutions by themselves. The materials show the seniors the error of their ways and allow for independent rectification. Caregivers can help seniors when required. The seniors learn their capabilities when they complete tasks and activities independently. When a senior is aware of their abilities, they will feel much more confident approaching challenges in the future.

Montessori Is Consistent

Montessori Methods are popular worldwide and have been successfully used as a form of education for over a century. Montessori has stayed the same as the methods work, and there has never been a reason to change. The Montessori approach is used on each senior depending on their level of mental capabilities. The methods always stay the same but are presented to suit a senior's current needs.

Each Senior Is Approached as an Individual

In Montessori, all seniors are observed and dealt with individually. Seniors are not forced to do anything that they don't want to do. They are gently guided towards activities and materials that interest them. They are always presented with opportunities that are appropriate to their level of development. The aim is to give each senior the chance to reach their full potential in all aspects of life.

Seniors Find It Easier to Understand

When a senior is filled with information without reason or explanation, they find it very hard to understand and remember, since they have not associated this information with any visual or mental interpretation. Seniors find it hard to absorb information that they do not understand. In Montessori, the senior can use materials and activities in various subjects to help them understand cause and effect. When a senior finds the answers to their questions, they start to link information together and set foundations for further development.

CHAPTER 3

ENVIRONMENT

Here are some suggestions to put into practice immediately to prepare the environment in a Montessori style with your senior from 65 years old. Indeed, an essential point to help the senior to be autonomous and therefore to oppose them as little as possible lies in the preparation of the environment. In an environment that's not suitable, it is impossible for them to take care of themselves, creating great frustration due to the gap between their desire to be great and the inability to be alone.

The more user-friendly the environment is for them; the greater will be their desire to use it and be with you. The environment also needs to be tidy, nice, and clean, so that they can find and put things back. If you don't create a place to hang used hats, jackets, and clothes, it is very likely that they will all end up on the ground.

Their bedroom will be prepared with care so that it is a welcoming place with light and bright colors—tidy and pleasant. Create a reading corner that is attractive and comfortable in their bedroom, or in the common place where you usually read. Their books must be placed so that they can access them. Leave a selection for them that you will change when you see their interests change.

The seniors must have access to their own clothes in order to learn how to dress on their own. Drawers are excellent allies where you can glue a figure of what each drawer contains so that you can take and put away your clothes. It is essential that the senior has a table with a chair of their size at their disposal in order to work in comfort and autonomy. Choose light furniture that can move on its own, preferably in neutral and light colors. So, keep their room clean, thinking that they will often be lying on the floor or carpet.

If you usually spend most of your time in a specific room of the house, such as the living room, also create a neat little corner there with some games and activities and provide them with a place where they can sit comfortably or lie on the ground and play while remaining together to the rest of the family.

From the bedroom to the entrance, passing through the kitchen and the bathroom: the tips for transforming the house in Montessori style. Transforming a senior-friendly home according to the Montessori Method is easy; it requires few precautions and above all, the desire to get involved by experimenting with a different point of view, that of the little one. The first thing to do is to create a stimulating and welcoming environment for them, suitable for movement and that allows them to be able to move independently, educating them that freedom is fundamental. The more they are given the opportunity to do so, the more they can learn. It is good to remove dangerous (or precious) objects and perhaps replace them with others that are still of interest to them and that can be put in the mouth without danger.

The Environment

Safety first. Check that there are no detergents, medicines, or anything else potentially dangerous is out of their reach. The senior grows, the attentions change, and the needs and the surrounding environment also change. To help them, open the doors of the house, in case they do not reach the handles, you can attach a ribbon so that by pulling it they can lower them and open the door.

From the age of 65, the environment must not be created to prevent damage, but so that the senior can use it and learn to do it in the right way by developing the necessary dexterity. Make sure that the environment is orderly, that there is a place for everything and that everything has a place to respond to the senior's inner need for order.

The Bedroom

The senior's bedroom is the first Montessori room, and special precautions must be dedicated to it. The right brightness, the neutral tones of the walls, and a few attractive and quality objects are the starting point for creating a space within which you and your senior will spend a lot of time together.

Create a simple and tidy place divided into four rooms: one for bedtime (unless they sleep with you), one for changing, one for eating, and one for activities. Do not forget to indulge the senior's personality and allow them to play and have fun independently. For the first months, the activity area will be represented by a soft carpet, resting on the ground, near a wall where you will have placed a mirror in which the senior can see their own image.

Leave them no more than two, three games available at a time, replacing them when you see that they have lost interest in their eyes. Finally, put a reproduction of a work of art (which you will change from time to time) at their eye level, so that the senior can observe it.

The Entrance

It is important that the senior learns the order to make recommendations or to create a space with a stool suitable to its size where it can sit down to put on and take off their shoes. An easily accessible place to store the shoes must be provided in the shoe cabinet, alternatively, a basket. The jacket must be attached to a hanger that the senior can easily reach in total autonomy.

The Kitchen

Even in the kitchen, everything that can be useful to the senior must be at their height and easily accessible. You can organize a drawer or door, accessible to the senior, where they can store the dishes so that he can help themselves to eat. Prepare a dedicated space where they can find the necessary snack when they are hungry. Depending on the senior's height, you can use a simple riser to allow them access to the kitchen counter and sink or use a learning tower. They are easily found on the market, or you can also build them yourself. Choose lifts that are lightweight and that the senior can move on their own to access what they need.

The Bathroom

As with all other rooms in the house, the bathroom must also be made to measure and within reach of the senior. In the bathroom, place a small step to help them reach the sink, where they can find a small bar of soap or a liquid soap dispenser. Provide them with a toothbrush and comb that they can pick up, use, and put back on their own.

In case they do not reach the height of the mirror, put a lower mirror where they can see themselves. Even in the bathroom, as at the entrance, put a hanger to store the wipe once used. Alternatively, you can use the bidet as your personal "sink" by providing it with soap and a small mirror, alongside a cabinet where you can store the other items needed for the toilet. To let them wash themselves, pour some shampoo and shower gel into two small bottles so that they can do it themselves using a limited amount of product.

Three Reasons to Choose Montessori

There are many ways you could choose to educate your senior, so why choose Montessori? There are many benefits of Montessori education, and Montessori Methods have been used worldwide for decades. Here are some reasons why you should choose to educate your senior using Montessori techniques:

Seniors Are Observed and Given Opportunities That Suit Their Level of Aging

In traditional homes, seniors are taught using the same method. They are expected to learn at the same pace as one another and receive similar results. It simply does not work, as every senior is different, and every senior has individual requirements for their age. If you teach a group of seniors at the same level, those that fall behind find will find it hard to keep up. Those that are ahead can find it hard to pay attention when they are not learning anything new. Either way, it can affect a senior's confidence. Montessori environments allow for a senior to progress depending on their current level of development. Seniors can work alongside one another, at their own pace, with their own choice of study. The seniors are all individually observed. From these observations, they are presented with the environment and materials suitable for their stage of development.

Limited Rewards Help Seniors Learn Self-Discipline and Self-Satisfaction

Seniors do not benefit from being praised for everything they do. A senior that receives rewards for every accomplishment will find it hard to accept critique. In Montessori, there are no rewards. Everything a senior learns is left for them to appreciate. They feel a sense of self-satisfaction when they complete a task and learn to recognize their hard work. Rather than expecting a reward, seniors find personal joy from their successes. They see how their skills contribute to making life easier and more understandable. They realize that they are bettering themselves as people. When you praise a senior in Montessori, it is specific to what they are doing. For example, you could say, "I like how much detail you included in your artwork." You are not offering rewards or compliments for their work; instead, you show admiration for their determination.

Montessori Helps Seniors Figure Out Who They Are

Seniors can recognize their abilities when they experience trial and error. Allowing a senior to come up with their own solutions, instead of helping them solve their problems, can develop their sense of independence. They feel confident when they figure things out for themselves. A Montessori environment provides materials that allow seniors to see the error of their ways visually. They have the freedom to choose their materials and activities, which means they can make choices based on instinct. In Montessori, seniors can learn naturally and explore their interests, figuring out what they like and dislike.

CHAPTER 4
7 Montessori Activities for the Elderly

There are different types of Montessori activities that aid in senior mind improvement. Eye-hand coordination activities are useful because they help seniors improve their sight. They also increase strength and enable them to age into a responsible individual. Hand-eye coordination exercises allow the eyes to guide the hands in the right movement. Eye-hand coordination is vital because it helps the senior at many levels. This is because the eye directs the hand in forming letters and letting them stay in line. Eye-hand coordination activities are recommended because they help the seniors focus on what they are doing. The eye is the one that guides the senior, and this eliminates distractions. Eye-hand coordination activities are useful because they help in reading. Coordination skills help seniors to develop eye-tracking skills, which are useful in reading. They can also acquire eye-tracking skills from games and other interesting activities. Coordination skills come in handy in sports. They are also vital in life as seniors use them to stack towers or build with Lego. Having known the benefits of eye-hand coordination, seniors should be provided with the necessary materials to nurture such skills.

There are several activities that seniors can engage in to develop eye-hand coordination skills. They can partake in suspended ball activities. To make this exercise simpler, suspend a ball in a net to avoid chasing it while the senior practices coordination skills. You can use a net bag, pop the ball in, and knot it. Tie it to reach a rope length, and it should be long enough to reach the senior's chest.

Suspend the ball away from you. You can push and catch or bat it. Another activity that seniors can do to improve their eye-hand coordination skills is rolling a ball. This exercise is amazing for seniors because it is fun and different from usual activities. To do this exercise, let the senior lie with lets apart, and proceed to roll the ball to them. Ask the senior to stop the ball before it hits the body. The senior needs to focus keenly on the ball as you roll it to stop it from hitting the body. Moreover, they will coordinate the hands to stop the ball before it hits the body.

Another exercise seniors can participate in to improve eye-hand coordination is passing and tossing the ball. It requires a lot of concentration for the senior to pass or toss a ball with both hands. Start by giving the senior a light object to pass and move to heavier ones when they become stronger. For seniors to master coordination skills, they need to practice for some time. Play forms an essential part in the development of eye-hand coordination skills. The secret to improving coordination skills lies in doing exercises that do not focus on objects or destinations, but the space in between.

Another activity that seniors can do to improve their coordination skills is bouncing a ball. Let the senior hold a racket in front of them, with the palm facing up. Hold the racket with them if they are unable to do it alone at first. Take a ball and tell the senior to bounce it as many times as possible without missing it. Have them repeat this exercise many times throughout the day. A wall ball exercise is another great way to improve eye-hand coordination. It is amazing because the senior cannot do it alone. To do this exercise, tell them to take a ball and throw it in front of the wall, and catch it. Repeat this exercise and move far from the wall, the more they practice. Jigsaw puzzles are also great for improving eye-hand coordination skills. They can improve fine motor skills and sharpen visual perceptions.

Moreover, jigsaw puzzles improve the senior's memory and help them set goals. Seniors need to choose an age-appropriate puzzle. Choosing a difficult puzzle leads to frustration and can demotivate the senior from using puzzles in the future. There are several options to choose from to enhance eye-hand coordination skills.

Practical life activities should be encouraged because they give seniors life skills. These are skills that may not be acquired in the classroom. These activities help the seniors to understand the world and find their place in it. Practical life activities are important because they prepare them for the real world.

The best way to cultivate a healthy lifestyle is to start young. There are various movement exercises that seniors can do to stay active. Music is a great alternative for seniors who have a difficult time finding what they like. There is no doubt that music is an effective tool for learning. Exposing seniors to music has profound benefits, such as boosting their confidence, boosting brain power, and promoting social skills. Studies have proven countless benefits of music and movement to seniors. The best way to get the seniors to move around is to play music. This is because music empowers and motivates them through the workout routine. Combining music and movement is a great way to help them develop gross and fine motor skills.

Cognitive Skills

Riddles

Those who were incapable of solving the Riddle of the Sphinx paid for their ineptitude with their lives. The Sphinx, as legend would have it, devoured anyone daring to enter the city of Thebes, which she guarded night and day, who could not answer her riddle. Oedipus did answer her riddle. Although he was not killed by the Sphinx, we know what happened to him nonetheless. And all this over a riddle!

Now it's your turn to solve riddles. As always, these will start off easy. A hint is provided for the first five puzzles in the form of the first letter of the required word.

- It flies, yet it has no wings. It can be long and short, yet it is not a measuring stick. It can be put into a capsule, but it is not a medicine. What is it? (Hint: The first letter is **t.**)
- What is it that everyone uses more than you do, yet it belongs to you? (Hint: The first letter is **n.**)
- Its colors are red, blue, purple and green. You can easily see that. But you can't touch it or even reach it. What is it? (Hint: The first letter is **r.**)

Riddles in Myth and Legend

Samson's life ended in calamity over a riddle he posed to the Philistines, as those who are familiar with the Bible story can attest. Also, in the Old Testament, Josephus writes that Hiram (the king of Tyre) and Solomon waged a riddle contest against each other. The ancient Greek priests and priestesses, known as oracles, were wont to express their more ominous prophecies in the form of riddles.

Riddles also appear in narratives. In the fairy tales of the Brothers Grimm, in the Mother Goose nursery rhymes, and in J. R. R. Tolkein's *The Lord of the Rings*, among many others. And let's not forget pop culture, where the Riddler, of Batman comic fame, is a well-known villain who always has a riddle handy.

- It can be put on scales, but it is not a substance. It is blind, but it is not a human being. What is it? (Hint: The first letter is **j.**)
- It can be Promethean. It can be infernal. And, of course, it can be eternal. What is it?
- It can be golden, but it is not a metal. It can be of one's eye, but it is not a human organ. Some would even say it is forbidden. What is it?

Drawing and Weighing Puzzles

These are classics. In other puzzle books, these might be classified under different rubrics. They are included here, but simply because they are based on a specific pattern or principle and thus involve a specific kind of reasoning combined with a touch of insight.

In a box, there are twenty balls, ten white and ten black. They all have the same indistinguishable texture to them. With a blindfold on, what is the least number of balls you must draw out of the box to be sure of having a pair of balls that matches in color—two white or two black? That is, you cannot assume luck drawing out two white balls or two black balls in a row. You must remove enough balls to guarantee a color match, even if you have some left over when you take your blindfold off.

Now, let's increase the number of balls in the box to thirty. Ten white, ten black, and ten green. What is the least number of balls you must draw out of the box this time (with a blindfold on, of course) to be sure of having a pair of balls that matches in color—two white, two black, or two green?

Let's increase the number of balls in the box again to forty. Ten white, ten black, ten green, and ten red. With your blindfold back on, what is the least number of balls you must draw out of the box this time to be sure of having a pair of balls that matches in color—two white, two black, two green, or two red? Moreover, can you see a general pattern emerging from having solved three puzzles of this type?

Let's increase the number one more time to fifty, but this time, let's vary the number of colored ball sets. In the box, there are two white, eighteen black, sixteen green, four red, and ten orange balls. Again, what is the least number of balls you must draw out of the box this time (blindfolded) to be sure of having a pair of balls that matches in color—two white, two black, two green, two red, or two orange? Does the new proportion of balls affect the outcome?

If there are six pairs of black gloves and six pairs of white gloves in a box, all mixed up, what is the least number of draws that are required, with a blindfold on, to guarantee a matching pair of black or white gloves? In this case, a pair consists of one left-hand and one right-hand glove of the same color

Crossing Puzzles

Puzzles involving coins, balls, and so on that are to be moved in a certain way and puzzles that involve crossing a river under given circumstances have been around since time immemorial. All require the use of clever reasoning. The puzzles here include some real classics.

A traveler comes to a riverbank with a wolf, a goat, and a head of cabbage. To his chagrin, he notes that there is only one boat for crossing over, which can carry no more than two passengers—the traveler and either one of the two animals or the cabbage. As the traveler knows, if left alone together, the goat will eat the cabbage and the wolf will eat the goat. The wolf does not eat cabbage. How does the traveler transport his animals and his cabbage to the other side intact in a minimum number of back-and-forth trips?

Three wives and their husbands come to a river. The small boat that will take them across holds only two people. To avoid any compromising situations, the crossings are to be so arranged that no woman shall be left alone with a man unless her husband is present. If any man or woman can be the rower, how many crossings are required?

Memorizing Game Cards

One of the keyways we can use memory is by remembering game cards. This is a technique that is often employed by poker players or casino dealers in Las Vegas. An essential aspect of remembering cards is through making word associations with images. When you can remember a number, you can put an image to it and easily remember it, which will help you when you're playing the game with others. Let's look at some tricks you can use when you're memorizing playing cards.

Using Peg Words

One important way to remember cards is by using peg words, such as H2 for hen, which has two hearts, H3 for ham, which has three hearts, and H4 for hair, which has four hearts. When you can assign a word to the card or number, it will help you remember much better. Let's look at the basics of pegs in a card game.

- Spade has one point
- Heart, which has two halves
- Club has three leaves
- Diamond has four points

You can use each of these numbers for the different suits and then you can memorize each card associated with that suit. For example, if you have a diamond that has 1, you might associate it with 401, and then you can make the association with that, as you're memorizing the cards. Instead of saying 1 of diamonds, you can use this number, which makes it a lot easier to recall.

Take an Imaginary Walk Somewhere

You will take a walk through a familiar place, like your home or an office building. As you do a walk through this place, you will become intimately familiar with 52 spots that you can apply to your mental journal (*How to Memorize a Deck of Cards*, 2019). Then, choose 5 rooms where you want to store the information. For example, you could choose your bedroom, bathroom, kitchen, or home office.

In each of the five rooms, memorize 10 items of furniture. Imagine you've stepped into the place, and you scout out the 10 furniture items. Then, look at them clockwise in your memory. Move around in the room and visualize each item. Then, repeat all these items in your head. Try to lock in these items in your memory by repeating them as much as possible. Finally, add two pieces of furniture that will complete the 52 cards.

Make the 52 Cards into 52 Famous People

You will remember cards more vividly when you assign a picture to them. Why not try imagining 52 celebrities and matching them to the 52 cards? This will make memorization much easier

Find Ways of Remembering Each Card

Now, think of a way you can remember each card by looking at them as if they were male or female. For example, kings are male and are half of a celebrity couple. And queens are the female half of the couple. Jacks are male and they are bachelors. So, you could say that Jacks are famous male bachelors (*How to Memorize a Deck of Cards*, 2019).

The highest numbers in the deck are 10 and 9. They represent powerful people. 10 is the most famous woman. And 9 is the most powerful man. Number 8 looks like an hourglass and can resemble a body. Therefore, 8 and 9 represent the body of the man and woman. For example, 8 represents a woman with a fabulous physique and 9 is a man who has a great body. Number 5 and 6 sound like fight and sex, so this couple will be controversial. 6 will represent a woman who is controversial and 5 is a controversial man.

Now, think of the number of actors or actresses who have starred in a famous trilogy. Number 4 will be the number of women who have starred in a trilogy and 3 will be the men who have been in a trilogy. Imagine those in your mind.

Practical Life Activities

Practical life activities are the daily drills aimed at helping a senior to understand the events in their daily life and learn how to do basic things in a resolute manner. Additionally, practical life activities help in enhancing the growth and development of a senior by aiding in the harmonization of movement of body parts and imparting a sense of independence and order. As a result, a senior is enabled to adapt to the environment and develop a good intellectual understanding of the surroundings and concentration skills.

Preliminary Activities

Preliminary activities are often the baseline activities that are introduced in the first days of the senior. They are important for the orientation of the seniors to the environment. These activities are always done with definite materials that do not require an introduction. Ideas made known are grouping, pairing, matching, and three-dimensional relations; the content is mostly dimensions and outlines. The materials help develop coordination and physical skill. Preliminary activities can be categorized into two. The first category involves activities that isolate motion related to certain objects in the environment or movements within the environment. The second category of activities is one that isolates a specific but important movement from a more complex order of work.

Setting Down

Make sure that you remind the seniors about the activity you are about to teach. The introduction makes the alert and ready to observe and learn.

Step by Step

- Carefully lower your arm towards the tabletop.
- Let the book rest on the table by removing letting grasp of it.
- At this point, ask the seniors to do what they have observed.

Opening and Closing a Door

You are required to draw the attention of the senior towards a door with a door handle. The handle must be at a height that the senior can reach for this activity to be effective.

Step by Step

- Grasp the handle and turn it downwards.
- Pull the door gently towards you or away from you depending on the direction that it turns to when opening.
- Once the door is open, and the senior has observed carefully, push the door gently to close it.
- Invite the senior to open and close the door by following the steps you have shown.

Rolling and Unrolling a Carpet

The activity is essential in developing coordination, movement of the body, and attentiveness. You only need a carpet and the attention of your senior for the activity.

Step by Step

- Lay down the carpet on the floor.
- Put your palm beneath the carpet and roll it slowly, showing the senior all the motions.
- To unroll the carpet, put your hand on one edge of the carpet and slide it open on the floor.
- Invite the senior to participate in rolling and unrolling the carpet.

Folding Clothes

For the exercise, you require pieces of clothes and a cloth basket. Prepare for the presentation by inviting the seniors to the workstation. Place the cloth basket where all the seniors can observe clearly. Remind the seniors that they are about to learn folding clothes by observing how you fold the clothes. The purpose of the exercise is to help them learn well-developed control of their hands in preparation for geometry by intuitive engagement in, and observation of, the lines of the folded clothes. The activity is recommended for seniors aged between 2 ½ to 4 years.

Step by Step

Note: Make sure that every senior has a tray of cloth.

Folding

- Place a flat piece of cloth on a tabletop.
- Have your palm underneath the cloth and fold into half
- Repeat the second step until the cloth cannot be folded anymore.
- Slowly slide out the palm from beneath the folded clothing.

Unfolding

The easiest way to unfold a piece of clothing is by pinching one corner and lifting it. The clothing will unfold automatically. Alternatively, you can slide your palm into the half fold of the clothing and lift the other half towards you until it is flat on the tabletop. Once the activity is complete, and all the seniors have folded and unfolded their pieces of clothes, replace the clothes in the basket.

Opening and Closing a Bottle

The exercise is intended to strengthen the hands and wrists of seniors and help them learn how to handle the task of opening and closing a bottle well by themselves. The main point of interest is to feel the rotational effect of the lid of a bottle when it is opening and closing.

Step by Step

Opening

- Wrap the lid of a closed bottle with your fingers.
- Twist the lid of the bottle in an anticlockwise

direction until it opens.

- Raise the lid for the seniors to observe.

Closing

- Hold the bottle in one hand
- Wrap your fingers around the lid and replace on the opening of the bottle
- Twist the lid in the clockwise direction until it cannot move anymore.
- Lift the bottle up for the seniors to observe.
- Let the seniors try their hands in opening and closing their bottles.

Turning the Pages of a Book

The gentleness required in this activity helps in creating awareness among seniors on how to treat their books.

Materials: A book, a chair, and a table.

Step by Step

- While seated at a central position, put the thumb of your hand on the edge of the book cover.
- Lift the cover slightly just enough to put your palm beneath it.
- Move the cover page to tilt leftwards. Do the same for other pages.

Siting and Standing from a Chair

The exercise requires a chair and the attention of the seniors. Slowly demonstrate to the seniors how to seat gently on the chair and how to stand up from it. It is purposeful in aiding the senior to advance the necessary movement skills to avoid missing the chair.

Self-Sustaining Activities

Activities that enhance care for oneself are highly regarded in a Montessori classroom. It is essential to help the seniors identify their physical needs and learn how to meet those needs. However, it is recommended that we slow down and help the seniors do certain things on their own. This creates a sense of impartiality and builds self-esteem among seniors.

- **Make the materials easy to get to (the accessibility factor):** the most important aspect of helping a senior to care for themselves is by availing the essential materials and making them easy to access. Always try to keep the resources required for the physical care of the senior within their reach.
- **Take your time:** caregivers need to bid their time when dealing with seniors. Yes, it takes a lot of time for them to master the skills required to do things on their own. A lot of patience is required to guide them. Give them room to grow and develop the skills. Take your time and think about it as a time investment. It takes longer now, but when they finally learn, they make it easier for you.
- **Create awareness:** at this early age, seniors are not aware of certain aspects of their lives and may fail to notice the need to help themselves. Make your choice familiar with the skills you would wish

them to possess.

Hand Washing

There are many ways to integrate this activity into the lives of your seniors. First, you can start by providing wet wipes or hand towels and letting the seniors help wipe their hands after activities that make their hands dirty, before eating and after having a meal, etc. The second method involves teaching them how to wash their hands using soap and water. Note to use warm water to encourage the seniors to wash their hands most of the time. Show your seniors the necessary hand washing steps like wetting their hands in water, applying soap to the wet hands, rinsing the hands with clean water, and finally using a towel to dry their hands.

Dressing and Undressing

A Montessori caregiver is encouraged to help the independence of the seniors by helping them to learn how to dress and undress on their own. Provide a set of a buckle, considerably on a dressing frame. The end goal is for the seniors to acquire the skills needed to buckle or unbuckle on their own. The activity helps coordinate movement and create self-awareness.

To unbuckle, pinch the strap and pull it out with one hand as the other hand holds the mettle buckle loop. Buckle up and let the senior unbuckle. If successful, proceed to buckle. For the buckling lesson, pinch the tip of the strap and guide it with your hand through the loop. Pull the strap to fit the desired size. Position the pin into the hole on the strap that corresponds to it. Invite the senior to demonstrate the activities simultaneously.

Hooking and Unhooking

Some of the clothes we use on our seniors have the hook and eye. It is, therefore, important to show them how to hook and unhook safely. The activity supplements dressing and undressing in seniors. For the exercise, you need a pair of hooks and an eye mounted on a dressing frame or a piece of cloth in the house that has a hook and eye.

To hook, hold the hook in one hand and the eye in the other hand. Insert the hook into the eye slowly for your senior to observe effectively. To unhook, put the hook side on one hand and the eye side on the other slide the hook slowly out of the eye. Invite your senior to do the exercise as you observe to correct an error.

Brushing Hair

For this activity, make sure that a smooth hairbrush and a mirror are easy to get to. Show your senior how to brush their hair from the top downwards checking in the mirror to find out if the hair is neatly done.

Getting a Drink

It is important to make water easy to get to for your senior. Set out a specific station for a water jug and glass, notably on a table or shelf in the kitchen where they reach. As they grow old, they can use the water dispenser. Putting a towel or a mop in the station is essential as it helps the seniors to dry water spills on the table and floor.

Preparing Food

This activity is very important in refining fine motor dexterities and attentiveness and is very engaging to the seniors. Start by showing your seniors how to prepare simple food such as peeling a banana. As time goes by, you can show them how to spread butter on a slice of bread. Seniors can also learn by arranging spoons in a container

First Aid

Simple first aid skills can be mastered and done by seniors. If the injuries are not serious like a simple scratch, show the senior how to clean the affected area using alcohol swabs. You can place the alcohol swabs and first aid bands in a tray at a place that is easy to get to.

Applying Lotion and Sunscreen

This activity can be very simple if you show the senior what to do. Provide a small bottle of lotion or sunscreen and show the senior how to squeeze the bottle gently and apply the lotion. Do not forget to provide a mirror for this activity.

Shoe Polishing

Showing your senior how to polish their shoes refines concentration through preparation and order and the advancement of a well-developed control mechanism of the hands. Take on the steps one by one, as the senior observes. Alternatively, you can provide two pairs of materials each so that the senior does what you are doing concurrently. Do not forget to put on an apron and help your senior put on one too as the activity can get messy for starters. Once you are done, put everything away in its rightful place and invite the senior to wash their hands.

Zipping and Unzipping

As part of showing your senior how to dress, zipping and unzipping is a very important skill in the development stage of their life. For starters, you should provide a dressing frame with a zipper to see and practice easily. Commence the presentation by placing your thumb beneath the zipper and your index finger over the zipper so that the fingers nip with the zipper in between. Move the zipper up and down as you tell your senior that that is how to zip and unzip. Since you are using a frame, remember to ask the senior to show you where a zipper is in their clothes. The activity is vital in enhancing coordination of movement.

Care for the Environment

Our planet should be taken good care of to ensure that the limited resources last longer to benefit us all. There is no recommended age to start teaching your senior how to take care of the environment. A Montessori senior is urged to impart the skills to reduce, reuse, and recycle to help maintain a cleaner and greener environment.

The activities that foster care for the environment are meant to help the seniors take part in making their surroundings clean and relate freely with the things in the environment; it can nurture the interaction of the seniors with the environment. Additionally, as they interact with their environment, the activities refine their sense of responsibility. Introduce the undertakings slowly and integrate more complex ones as the senior grows. In no time, you will realize that the seniors can make a remarkable difference in your home.

Outdoor Sweeping

Helping your senior to develop environmental awareness is the primary aim of this activity. It also improves the controlled movements of the body. Using a broom show the senior how to sweep, moving the dust to collect in one place before scooping the dust and putting it in a bin. Remember to put on gloves when picking up the dust. Ask your senior to sweep another section of the driveway.

Washing a Chalkboard

The materials required for this activity are a sponge of a piece of cloth, water in a bowl, and dry cloth. The purpose of the activity is to aid the seniors to identify the buildup of chalk dust on the chalkboard and show them how to clean it independently. For the presentation, soak the sponge in the bowl of water; squeeze the sponge to drip off excess water. Place the sponge on the chalkboard and wipe the board clean. Once the entire board is wiped clean, dry it using the extra piece of cloth. Let your senior take their turn in doing the cleaning.

Polishing Glass

Nothing can beat the act of lending a hand in doing the household chores. Well, this is made possible by teaching them how to do simple tasks like polishing glass. Using a piece of cloth, apply some polish to the mirror and let it dry. Once dry, remove the polish by wiping the mirror surface with a clean wet cloth. Dry the mirror and let your senior polish another mirror. Put everything away and wash your hands as they do the same after the activity. It is crucial to put on an apron for this and other cleaning exercises.

Setting a Table

You are required to set aside a table for this activity. Alongside the table have a stool with a mug, a bowl, a small serving dish, a table knife, a teaspoon, and a tablemat. The activity not only creates a sense of independence but also integrates the seniors into the social structure.

Ask your senior to pick one object at a time and show them, by pointing, where you want it placed. Once the table is set, ask the senior to help carry food to the table. Remember to start with light and cold items only.

Dusting a Table

The required materials are a duster or a piece of cloth. Place the duster on the tape and wipe the entire top of the table. You can also add soapy water to dip the duster in and use it to wipe the table. In case you used water, rinse the duster, and use it to dry the table. Alternatively, you can use a separate dry cloth to dry the table. Ask the senior to do the same.

Arranging Flowers

Your senior can absorb how to cut the stems of flowers and arrange them neatly in a flower vase. Pour water in a vase until it is ¼ full. Using a pair of scissors, cut the tip of the stem of the flower such that the remaining tip fits nicely in the vase. Ask the senior to cut the other tips and put the cut flowers in the vase. Use flowers that are just enough for the vase. Once the flowers are neatly arranged, tell your senior to move the vase to a desired spot in the house. Clean the workstation.

Grace and Courtesy

It is fundamental that the senior gets acquainted with the social structures in place to understand their surroundings well. The activities on elegance and good mannerism build the vocabulary of the senior along with helping in improved awareness of the surroundings and the receptiveness of the people around them. As a result, the senior gets oriented to the natural and social space. It is your role to use the right words, clear-cut activities, and present steps as you assist the senior to develop a good indulgent of themselves as well as others. At the right time, the senior will get a grip of the how's, the when's, and the where's to apply the terms for a more satisfying life for others and them. In the long run, the senior learns to integrate good mannerisms into their life on a daily basis.

Introducing Oneself

Show your senior how to introduce themselves when they meet someone new, for instance, "Hello, my name is Leah." Remind them that they can shake your guests' hands while introducing themselves.

Greeting a Person

For this activity, you need to show your seniors how to greet each other while maintaining eye contact. You can shake their hands as you say "hello Lisa" or "hello Jimmy" and teach them how to respond. Other great words to use for this activity are "good morning," "good afternoon," etc.

Showing Gratitude

It is important to teach your senior to show gratitude and appreciation by saying thank you. Ask them always to say thank you if someone gives them something or does something nice to them. You can integrate this activity during meals when you pass the salt or help them tie a napkin.

Interrupting

As much as it is never polite to interrupt someone, we sometimes must get their attention, and in so doing, we should use the politest way. In the case of dialogue, you should teach how to take turns politely. Words such as "excuse me, can I have your attention for a moment" or "I'm sorry to interrupt, but really need to speak to you" are important to help the senior develop polite vocabulary when interrupting others.

Coughing

It is important that a senior knows what to do when coughing to avoid coughing on other people. For the activity, you should tilt your face slightly away from the senior, place your forearm close to your mouth, cough, then close your mouth before removing the forearm and turning to face the senior. Explain the steps to the senior and have them exaggerate a cough as they do what you have shown and explained

Yawning

What you need to do when teaching your senior how to yawn is already explained in the activity above (coughing). Just for clarity, you can repeat the explanations to the seniors and have them practice yawning the right way.

Walking on the Line

Walking on the line activity is a good exercise for this. The activity helps the senior to have better control of the body, improve stability and balance along with developing the action of the mind in controlling the movement of the body. For the activity, the line denotes a continuous path in the environment. The distance between the lines should be just wide enough to accommodate the shoes of the senior. The line should not be hidden or concealed. For a group, place your seniors on the line midway between each other. Ask them to walk in the line while maintaining the distance in between and to stop when you ask them to.

Hopping Over a Log

Hopping over a piece of the log may seem easy and simple, but the amount of concentration and coordination required to perform the task is essential in the development of the senior. Additionally, the energy level required to jump over, again and again, is enormous. The activity not only keeps the senior fit by enhancing the growth of muscles of the legs but also makes them sharp and attentive.

You can also challenge your seniors to walk on the log. This gives them the outdoor version of walking on the line and is an adventurous upgrade to the traditional walking on the line activity. The log activity requires additional balance as compared to the line.

The Silence Games

Everyone needs a moment of tranquility and peace of mind to have a rest and meditate. Endless noise may lead to petulance, obstruction, misperception, and even drowsiness. Dr. Montessori observed that a profound level of consciousness and thoughtfulness could help in creating a more advanced and elusive environment. For this purpose, the silence game was introduced.

During this activity, the seniors are expected to stay quiet. Staying quiet means that the senior must have great control of the movements of the body and connect with the mind. They must have a decent synchronization of body movement and the brain, possess a solid resolve and have pronounced responsiveness of the things and people in the surrounding.

Art, Craft, Music, and Movements Activities to Stimulate the Creativity

Through manual work and art, seniors perfect their movements, experience the joy of creating and are intellectually stimulated to know the principles of the technique. Their ability to appreciate the artistic value of objects is awakened: color, line, pattern, structure, design, and they become passionate observers of the world around them. From manual work and the practice of art, seniors learn the sense of their value in things and experience great inner satisfaction.

Senior Creativity Develops from Knowledge

The creative potential expands when the senior develops the ability to observe, learns to use tools effectively and efficiently, refines the movement of the fingers, and has the opportunity to admire examples and to have direct experiences.

It is a mistake to leave seniors to their "ignorance" in the belief that this frees them to be creative. Random creation is not art. True creativity is a conscious effort, planned, implemented with defined purposes. We must not be afraid to teach seniors what our best artists and craftsmen have learned before them. This does not mean that seniors are not able to manage the materials themselves, only that they must be told what the potential of the materials is.

We must teach our seniors what we have learned before them, knowing that this has a purpose. After learning the basics, the senior can go the distance and get great pleasure from manual and artistic work by realizing their creative ideas. But to develop creativity, a knowledge transfer is first necessary.

There is a way to use a particular tool to be able to make the most of it; improper use can damage the instruments and above all, leave the senior unsatisfied with their use. It is important to give them good tools to use, and materials that they can easily control and manipulate.

The scissors must cut well; a large set of colored pencils, in which there are many different shades of each color, will allow seniors to develop a more precise understanding of colors. Brushes must be of good quality and must be made available in a wide range of sizes to enable them to develop greater painting skills. Furniture and woodworking tools must be of adequate size for their build, but well designed and functional.

A 60- or 90-year-old senior can spend many hours hammering nails on a block of wood, but after this first phase in which they enjoy the simple experimentation of the technique, they want to do something to create a project that can be completed relatively quickly, like a simple plane.

Seniors should always be shown the techniques and procedures that true artists and craftsmen follow in their work. If you want to teach a senior the technique of watercolor painting, it is better to propose it on a slightly inclined sheet rather than on a vertical easel, where the color would slide in an uncontrolled way and the wet paper would curl.

Seniors must be taught the proper care and maintenance of tools: how to wash and dry brushes, etc. When walking with scissors, you have to teach them to hold them with the tip pointing downwards, when you have to move them to another, you have to teach them to do so by holding them out from the handle.

Normally, works are not displayed on the walls of the classroom, because the environment must be kept as quiet as possible, and the senior attention must be directed mainly towards learning materials and other objects of particular interest. Protecting the working environment is also very important. Seniors must wear aprons and must cover the desks with newspapers before using glue or paint colors.

Once the techniques have been learned, the teacher provides models that the seniors can create independently using their new skills, or they can create their own projects. It is important that initially the work can be completed in a short time, one or two lessons at the most. In addition to artistic and craft techniques, manual work can be addressed to the study of nature, physics, social studies, mathematics, music, and more.

Applied to the study of nature, manual work teaches you to be a passionate observer, to look at a spider's web, and draw your own conclusions...The study of geography is accompanied by the creation of maps and globes, and even art, in general, becomes geography cultural, for example, with the making of masks. Many manual activities can enrich the study of mathematics.

It is useful and interesting to tell seniors the stories of some of the great artists of the past and contemporary and to lead them to understand how each of these artists had to learn everything they are learning, before creating great works. They had to learn to grind the colors, to prepare the canvas, to make sketches; they had to spend years of apprenticeship before the master gave them permission to paint, even if only a part of a background or a tree.

It is important to have good art books in the home so that the senior can sit and look at them. They should be taught to place the book on the table and turn the pages carefully. Of course, today it is possible to visit all the great museums on the web. The computer, therefore, assists in the study of art and can help all of us to know and appreciate great art, become familiar with various artistic styles, and develop our sensitivity to the elements of design.

Montessori gave musical education an essential function, not just for intellectual development, but for the global education of the senior—also from the psychic point of view. It's now universally recognized that music is an essential element of an education that develops the principles of freedom, autonomy, collaboration, participation, respect, solidarity. Items that are in pacifist thought of Montessori and the elaboration of a "cosmic plane," synthesis of her educational philosophy

Montessori Neuroscience and Sensory Material

Today, thanks to neuro-scientific studies and diagnostic imaging, it is scientifically proven that the study of music, like that of figurative art, enriches the learner, not only making them able in the future to consciously enjoy the fruits of these languages, but developing in the intellectual, logical, intuitive, creative, and communicative skills, useful in various professional sectors.

Bruno Munari, a precursor of art teaching and creator of the first senior's workshop in a museum (Pinacoteca di Brera, Milan, 1977), declared himself close to Maria Montessori in his concept of autonomy of the small senior and of learning through the education of hand to "do." He agreed with Maria Montessori's concept of senior autonomy and, after having addressed for years to university or secondary home auditors, he finally concluded that only by educating seniors in kindergarten and primary homes to art still conditioned by a closed and distorted thought, one could hope for a better world in a few generations. From the same reflection on the future of human civilization, the concepts of cosmic education and education for peace, fundamental principles of Montessori educational philosophy, arose.

Maria Montessori was the first (1909) to talk about the musical education of small seniors in pre-home age; she created special practical-sensorial materials for ear education (bells and noise boxes) for the learning of musical notes and figures, already used in the first senior's houses at the beginning of the last century.

With the use of bells, Montessori makes listening and the nomenclature of sounds tangible, which will subsequently be used to introduce the senior to reading the notes, combining the graphic sign with a known sound. In fact, she considered sensory learning to be an indispensable step for the correct perception of abstract concepts such as sound, color, shape, to then proceed with the classification of the various parameters sensorially assimilated and their graphic reproduction.

The understanding of the language of music develops naturally, as it happens for the articulated language and subsequently for the mechanism of writing and reading, through methodical exercises (educational repetition). This slow maturation process is the necessary basis for subsequent formal education.

Music Education: Theory and Practice

Rousseau already argued that "the knowledge of notes is no longer necessary to be able to sing than the knowledge of letters is to be able to speak" (Rousseau, 1991).

It is a mistake, however, to limit oneself to "making music" by mere imitation without developing a real awareness of the use of the means of production. It would be like learning Italian by memorizing poems and stories without ever explaining the phonetics of the syllables and the construction of words. Today, we take the approach to read in kindergarten using whole words associated with images, but then we proceed with the learning of the alphabet and syllables; why do you stop at the first step with music? You can start by playing by imitation, but then you still need to learn the written musical language. The musical instrument must not be the purpose of the theoretical study of music, as it happened in the academic studies of the past (not so distant), but the means to encode its language.

As John Dewey (1977), Montessori's contemporary American philosopher and pedagogist, stated, "All art presupposes physical organs: the eye and the hand, the ear, the voice; and yet it is more than the technical expertise required by the organs of expression. It implies an idea, a thought, a spiritual translation of things." Ideas and thoughts that are expressed with a language, the musical one in our case, consisting of phonemes and graphemes like all the languages of man, who has always sought a graphic means of communication in all fields of knowledge.

"An initiation into the writing of musical notes is also possible in the senior ren's home. It hinges on the sensory exercises consisting in recognizing the musical sounds of the material of the bells... it is of great help, because it places the notes in a material form, like other objects for the education of the senses. All that remains is to match the note to its name...In this way, the senior, with the repetition of the exercise, comes to know with certainty the names related to the sounds...When the seniors begin to study the notes on the staff, therefore, they will as a written exercise of already known musical facts" (Montessori, 1999).

Materials similar to the "Montessori half" of the bells were later created and re-proposed for ear education in different teaching methodologies (Willelms, Orff), but it is only in Kodàly's methodology that we find an educational system, still today in use, for reading the notes on the staff: the mobile do.

Montessori has created some materials for the study of notes on the stave and for the study and transposition of scales, which find a widespread and detailed application in the books written by Anna Maria Maccheroni. One of the materials, consisting of a pentagram wooden blackboard, contains a brilliant intuition to make the reading of the notes simple and intuitive. Number staves and spaces in sequence and not as is usually done, 665 staves and 4 spaces. In this way, the senior visualizes the known sounds with the bells and understands the mechanism of the ordered succession of the sounds on the staff.

The mechanism of values is simplified and reduced to a simple sensory exercise of solid joints. The senior, through the different lengths of the wooden pieces, visualizes the different duration of the musical figures. As in the Montessori material used for the study of geometry, the fact of being able to handle the wooden pieces, arrange them freely, and observe the equivalence ratios, intensely attracts the senior's interest.

The Building Movement of Intelligence

The insights into Montessori's correct musical education, due to its vast scientific and pedagogical skills, are not limited to ear education and writing but involve all the sectors on which modern music teaching developed at the beginning of the century is based last.

Movement, a manifestation of life in every animated element of the planet, is considered an essential foundation of her education. From creating a "senior-friendly" environment to practical life activities, everything in the Montessori Method is movement. Movement ordered, guided, self-controlled, functional to the various activities, and certainly could not be missing in music education: "It is one of the mistakes of modern times to consider movement in itself as distinct from higher functions ... Mental development and the spiritual one can and should be helped by movement... Observations made on seniors from all over the world prove that they develop their own intelligence through movement; movement helps psychic development, and this development is expressed in turn with further movement and action" (Montessori, 1999).

Muscle training exercises to be performed on the wire, developed by Montessori to support the normal development of physiological movements, are of great use for the perception of rhythm, but also for the acquisition of correct breathing. The fluidity of body movement and the ability to move rhythmically are also effectively reflected in the development of vocal skills related to the respiratory rhythm; the correct intonation, in fact, is given by the coordination between breathing and sound emission. In the execution of the rhythmic gaits, it is also possible to begin to visualize the dynamics and the formal structure of a piece, it is possible to identify the instrumental timbre and the harmonic structure. The body thus becomes a means of representing, through movement, the different qualities of sound perception. The pitch, the duration, the intensity, the timbre, the pause, the phrase, and the musical form can be presented with musical games or even with traditional games adapted to the musical needs, stimulating in the senior greater attention and facilitating the understanding of the abstract concepts. Motor games can therefore have the same function that the Montessori sensory material has for the tangible representation of the physical qualities of objects.

As the Swiss teacher Jacques-Dalcròze, who mainly devoted himself to learning music through movement, confirmed to us, seniors following the trend of the music with steps, arm, and body movements, physically enter the piece and it perceives deeply, facilitating learning not only from a sensory and cognitive point of view but also from an emotional and psychic point of view.

Learning that is not purely intellectual but of self-education, self-knowledge, and exploration, which aims at the global formation of the senior. In fact, Montessori attributes an essential function to musical education, inherent not only to cognitive development but to the overall formation of the senior, also from a psychic point of view.

Montessori music education is aimed at stimulating the ability of attention and concentration, and therefore of learning, through listening; to develop manual skills with the use of tools, the articulation of language with nursery rhymes and songs; to achieve motor coordination and increase sociability with collective activities (dances, choir, orchestra); it is finally aimed at refining the taste and developing the critical ability and the control of emotions.

Vocal Education

If carried out correctly and competently, the constant practice of music education is, therefore, an invaluable source of resources for the harmonious growth of the senior, for the correct development and enhancement of multiple skills, as well as for the prevention and correction of various disorders of learning.

Given the affinity of sound production between language and singing, the exercises, described in detail by Montessori in the *Method of Scientific Pedagogy* to address the problems of breathing, emission, and articulation of a language can also be used in vocal education aimed at singing. Spoken language is closely related to singing, especially in the sensory age.

Montessori's operational proposals for correct language learning can be translated with a vocal education path that starts from the emission and musical intonation of a single sound, proceeds with the execution of single intervals, up to the realization of a short musical phrase.

Let's take, for example, the learning of the pitch parameter, following the Montessori procedure for the exercises with the sensory material. The first level of learning (identity) will be represented by the intonation of the unison; the second degree (contrast) from the pitch of an interval; the third and last degree (gradation) from the execution of a glissade or a scale.

Vocal reproduction, enriched with sound parameters (pitch, intensity, duration, and timbre), through rational gradualness of the stimuli, will favor the spontaneous progress of the senior.

The Cosmic Plan of Maria Montessori

The importance given to listening to music correctly, to musical education in the sensorial age, to the development of "musical intelligence" (self-education), to the development of spoken language closely connected to ear education (the mind of the senior), to the connection between listening education and correct vocal reproduction of sounds (the discovery of the senior), clearly show the Montessori vision: the musical activity must initially aim at the general formation of the senior, or contribute to their perceptive development, intellectual and creative, to the refinement of psychomotor faculties, to its social growth.

Music is an essential element in the perspective of an education that develops the principles of freedom, autonomy, but above all, collaboration, participation, respect, solidarity.

Sensory

Sensorial exercises are activities that sharpen up the senses of the senior—visual, auditory, tactile, olfactory, and gustatory. Seniors are predominantly open to refining their senses from the early age of 60, thus the importance of integrating the Montessori sensorial activities into their lives. The materials for these activities should be prudently designed to meet the basic principles set out by Dr. Maria Montessori. The Montessori sensorial materials aim at sharpening the senses of the senior to isolate and categorize materials distinctively in their environment. As a result, seniors are offered the chance to refine their intelligence regarding their surroundings.

The Montessori materials for refining the senses of seniors are specifically designed to:

- Help the senior to concentrate on isolating and identifying one quality at a time.
- Help the seniors in making their own corrections through the control of the error feature of the

material.

- Be physically attractive to call in the attention of the senior and help in maintaining focus and concentration.
- Be complete to help the senior go through the exercise to completion without having to pause in between the activity to find a misplaced part.

The materials are meant to turn theoretical ideas into substantial concepts. Nonetheless, the activities are not for a specific age group only. Monitor your seniors to know what they like and can do with ease because they develop at different paces.

The Coin Box

The coin box, or alternatively a domino box, enhances the hand-eye coordination of seniors. The material is designed with closing and opening slots and a hole in the top lid. Seniors are encouraged to fit certain objects in the box, which is opened when full to remove the objects. The disappearing and reappearing of the objects in and out of the box refine the concentration of them while the exercise of fitting objects into the hole improves accuracy.

Straws in a Cup

This activity involves putting colored straws in different containers, and the senior is invited to empty one at a time then put the straws back. To upgrade this exercise, a Montessori teacher is encouraged to use colored containers so that the senior can sort the straws according to colors when putting them back into the containers.

The Texture Basket

The texture tray or basket is a guileless activity that draws the attention of seniors into isolating the texture of materials. For the exercise, you are required to assemble different materials within the house and put them in a tray or basket. Invite the senior to feel the items by turning them over their hands and help them identify and isolate soft in one basket, and hard in a different one. Note that you should use simple words for this exercise.

Sound Cylinders

Sound cylinders are stress-free and the most charming materials to make and use. Seniors are always delighted to hear the different sounds produced by the cylinders. For the activity, use a control cylinder (say a yellow cylinder) to make the first sound by shaking it. Proceed to the next cylinder (say red). Shake the second cylinder and ask the senior to differentiate the sound from the first one. If the sound made is the same, the cylinders are put in one tray. Different sounds are put in separate trays. Invite the seniors to shake the cylinders and sort them according to the sound they make.

Color Marbles

This activity helps learners to differentiate colors. Seniors are invited to sort the marbles according to their colors and put them in a matching container. For a start, consider using simple or primary colors like red, yellow, white, and blue. In the presentation, remember to read out the colors of the marbles and the containers to the seniors as you match them. Once all the items are sorted, return them in a basket and invite your seniors to sort them. Additionally, you can upgrade this activity by increasing the range of colors and playing the color hunt game where you ask the senior to point a certain color in the house.

The Grain Box

This activity involves providing a variety of grains in different textures and sizes. Pool different grains like rice, beans, sand, stones, beads, etc. in a tray, basket, or box. Invite the senior to feel the texture, isolate the color, or isolate by size. For safety purposes, bear in mind the age of the senior and the grain provided. Always keep watch when carrying out this activity.

Spooning Ice

This activity is best suited for a hot day. You are required to provide ice in a bowl, an empty bowl, and a pair of tongs or a spoon. Show the senior how to scoop and lift ice with a spoon or tongs from one bowl into the other. Invite the seniors to try their hands on the activity. You can also ask the senior to feel the temperature of the bowl with ice and the empty bowl by wrapping their palms around it. This activity can be upgraded once the ice has melted by transferring the water from one bowl into the other using a syringe.

Sorting by Shape

For this activity, you should begin with a sample pack of simple shapes. For the start, provide the same shapes in the same color. At this point, your seniors can sort according to color. Advance by mixing the colors but maintaining the shapes. As you progress, introduce tracing the shapes on a piece of paper or board. For the presentation, name the shapes as you sort them first before inviting your seniors to do the same.

Fabric Board

This activity is very crucial in introducing texture to seniors. The activity involves presenting different fabric squares of different textures and inviting the senior to feel the difference. The textures are described in simple words like rough, soft, silky, etc. The senior is expected to match the fabrics with a similar texture. A homemade fabric board is made by cutting a piece of Styrofoam placard into a good size that fits into your basket or tray. Next, you glue different fabrics on each placard.

Simple Puzzle

This activity is essential in helping seniors to decode size and shape. The puzzle can be made by cutting a placard into one shape (say triangle), then drawing a puzzle in the shape. Cut out the drawn lines. Using a different piece of paper, draw a rough draft of the puzzle to be used as a control. Invite the senior to set up the cut pieces to form a complete shape seen on the control paper.

The Pink Tower

A complete pink tower consists of ten cubes of different sizes. For this activity, invite your senior to help you carry the cubes to your play station. Starting with the largest cube, construct the tower by piling the next largest cubes on top until all the cubes are used. In case the senior is not able to identify the next largest cube, help them by pointing out the cube.

Knobbed Cylinders

The knobbed cylinders are meant to help the senior differentiate height and diameter. Each block consists of roughly five cylinders decreasing in height and diameter. Show the senior how to carry the cylinders from one station to the other from the biggest to the smallest, which helps them in arranging the cylinders inside one another. Once the entire block is done, replace the cylinders in their original station.

Hanging Ball Activities

The set of activities in this section involves the use of a suspended ball. The ball is suspended to save you the time of chasing after missed balls as the exercise goes on. Set up the activity by putting a ball in a net and tying it with a rope. Suspend the ball on a hook, taking note to make it a level chest of the senior.

Racket and Ball

Help your senior to hit the suspended ball using a ratchet.

The point is to let the ball swing back and forth without missing a hit. Make the activity more challenging by using smaller balls and ratchets.

Push and Catch

The exercise requires the senior to push the ball and catch it as it swings back without missing or letting it bang against their body. This helps in refining concentration by carefully watching the ball swing from and to the hands. Upgrade to more challenging series by asking the senior to clap in between the catch and the push.

Hand-Eye Coordination Ball Games

Rolling a Ball

For this activity, sit opposite your senior. Have them sit with legs apart facing you. Roll the ball towards the seniors and ask them to catch the ball before it hits the body. The activity requires the senior to watch the rolling ball prudently and synchronize the hands into stopping the ball before it reaches the body.

Ball Relays

This activity is good for many seniors. The process requires that you provide a basin or basket full of balls. Make the person line up behind each other and place an empty basket or basin at a good distance from them. The exercise is picking a ball and running to the empty basket to put it there. Once the senior has put the ball in the basket, they run back and line up behind the other senior. This arrangement ensures that every senior has a turn to pick a ball, run, and put it in the other basket before coming back. Alternatively, they can line up in between the baskets with each senior keeping their position permanently. The senior closer to the basket with balls picks a ball and passes it to the next senior until the ball reaches the last senior who puts it in the empty basket. The activity goes on, once the other basket is full. To introduce more challenges, you can increase the distance between the seniors and ask them to toss the ball to each other or pass it overhead.

Tossing and Passing a Ball

This activity requires a lot of focus and concentration from the seniors to toss the ball overhead to one another without missing a catch or overpassing the ball. Position the seniors at a distance from each other. Give them a ball and ask them to toss it to each other. Increase the challenge by making circles on the ground and asking the seniors to stay in the circle when tossing and catching the ball.

Ball to Wall Toss and Rebound

This exercise follows the toss and catches activity. Once the seniors can pass the ball and catch it successfully, you upgrade to the ball-wall toss. Here, you show the senior how to toss a ball against a wall and wait for the rebound. The senior is expected to catch the ball as it rebounds back. Keep a record book to note down the number of successful tosses and catch before the ball falls. Always encourage your senior by offering a present every time they break their record.

Toss and Catch

One of the best hand-eye coordination activities is tossing the ball up in the air and catching it again. The exercise becomes more challenging when you introduce a circle that the senior is required to maintain standing in when tossing and catching the ball. Additionally, as your senior makes progress, encourage to toss higher.

Threading and Lacing

Another activity that enhances hand-eye coordination is stringing beads or lacing up cards. For a start, use beads with larger holes and reduce the size of the holes as the senior makes progress.

Tasting Bottle

This game is fundamental in helping seniors to isolate the four major tastes: salty, sweet, bitter, and sour. The game also helps improve the responsiveness of the senior to understand the connection between palate and scent. The activity involves presenting different bottles, each containing a different taste. The game is to taste the contents of the bottle and identify the taste.

Smelling Jars

Just like the taste bottles, the smelling jars are presented containing different scents. The senior is invited to smell each jar and differentiate the odor in them. This activity helps in building the ability of the senior to isolate the odor.

Matching Thermic Tablets and Bottles

The game is aimed at refining the thermic sense of the senior. The materials required are a set of thermic tablets in a box. For the presentation, remove all the tablets and place them on a tabletop. Invite the senior to feel the temperature of each with the back of the hand. Due to the difference in heat conductivity, the tablets will have a varying range of temperatures according to the material they are made of. For the game part, you can ask the seniors to close their eyes and feel one table. Ask the senior to find a tablet that feels the same without opening their eyes. Once done, have the seniors open their eyes and see if the tablets have been sorted correctly.

Maracas and Clatters

Put some maracas and clatters in an enclosed container. Invite the seniors to shake the container as they listen to the sound produced. You can put on some soft music for the seniors to shake the maracas and clatters along as they dance to the tunes.

Handprint Fall Tree Craft

This activity requires you to provide some bottles of paints and cotton swabs. Trace the outline of a tree on a piece of paper and let the seniors finish the leaves by dipping their fingers in paint and leaving prints on the image. Random prints can give the image a very appealing look.

The cotton swabs are used to clean the fingers to change to another color. After the activity, have your seniors wash their hands.

Paper Shape Collage

If your senior can draw, ask them to draw a random shape, say a triangle. Now have them introduce another shape in the triangle, say a circle. Tear colored papers of different colors and have your senior glue them to the image. Note that every shape should be given a different color of paper.

Creating Paper Plate Animals

Your senior can make paper plates by finger-painting them. To create the paper plate animals, guide them in fixing paper faces and limbs. The activity offers the environment for nurturing creativity and awareness of the surrounding.

Sticker Word Activity

This is among the simplest art and craft activities for the senior. Have them write their name on a manila paper (offer help if they cannot write on their own). Offer the senior a set of colored stickers to put on the name or word written. The stickers are put along the lines of the letters.

Colored Straw Necklace

For creativity and elegance, have your senior exercise this activity. Provide colored straws. Help them cut the straws using a pair of scissors to the desired size. The sizes may vary. Using the threading technique, you have taught the senior to thread the straws together and alternate the colors to give the necklace a beautiful look. For more designs, you can tie a knot after every straw. Join the ends of the string by tying them together. There, your senior just made a beautiful straw necklace.

Squirt Gun Painting

For this activity, hang a canvas on a board or use a sketching pad. Fill a squirt gun with watercolor and let your senior spray the canvas randomly. You should consider mixing the colors to give the paint an appealingly unique look.

Palm Painting

Have your senior dip the palm of their hands in paint and put a print on a piece of canvas. You can have a whole pad full of your senior's prints with a different color on each page. Apart from enhancing artistic skills, the activity provides a good source of seniorhood memory. This method can also be used to make fingerprint flowers.

Making Paper Rainbow

What is more beautiful than using craft to teach science? Here is how. Give your senior a card with the rainbow image as control. Now give them a set of colored paper strips. Let the senior arrange the colors of the rainbow as observed on the control card. You can add more learning lessons like naming the colors in the correct order and gluing the strips on a placard and hanging them in your senior's room.

Spray Paint Craft

Avail of a variety of spray paints. Write any word on a placard, cover the word with a tape such that the tape fits every letter and can be read. Invite your senior to spray paint the placard using different colors. Once done, remove the tapes to expose the word you had written.

CHAPTER 5
SENIORS WITH DEMENTIA/ ALZHEIMER'S DISEASE

Dr. Cameron J. Camp was the first American physician to use the Montessori Method from children to the elderly. The Montessori Method can have enormous benefits for people with dementia, as well as for their loved ones. Activities are generally easy to set up, can be modified according to a person's skills, and can be tailored to a person's background, occupations, and hobbies.

One way to help an older person is to incorporate activities based on the Montessori Method. This method emphasizes independence, freedom within limits, and respect for a person's natural psychological, physical, and social development. Developed in 1897 for children with special needs, this teaching process offers activities to help even dementia patients cope with daily life.

Montessori activities are simple, modifiable, and practical. Completion of activity can lead to a sense of accomplishment, reconnecting them with a part of their personal history. The shutdown of a brain with dementia is not like pulling the plug. It takes time. Taking energy away from the various departments (memory, language, movement...) becomes a job that is integrated and gradually completed as the days and life go by.

"The disease scrapes gram after gram off a one and a half kilo brain: the disease empties it with the teaspoon of a soft-boiled egg, without the emptied person perhaps noticing it in full and leaving it without the yolk."

The development of the disease is slow, and some atypical behaviors are noticed in the person from the very beginning. The most important of these behaviors, I believe, is certain bewilderment, sadness, restlessness. A state of perceived malaise, because the first to notice that something is changing is the people themselves.

I like to quote the metaphors used by Dr. Cameron J. Camp in his book *Living with Alzheimer's*, precisely to identify the main alarm bells, the first symptoms: the evil magic wand.

Short-term memories disappear. Mat Whitercross, an English director whose father fell ill with Alzheimer's, has defined this disease as a "cinematic pathology." Alzheimer's disassembles and reassembles film clips, mixes scenes, cuts off close-ups, and leaves the backgrounds intact (M. Farina - *Quando andiamo a casa?* Bur Editori). Scenes, memories, episodes that have just happened disappear from memory and the person loses all trace of them. They never happened, they are not there, they do not exist.

Dementia works like a backward time machine. In the early stages, you forget things or events that have just happened, as the disease progresses you may forget things that happened the day before, the week before, then the year before. Then a decade earlier. There is no point in arguing with a person with dementia because what is forgotten for us never existed for them.

Another problem that arises, different from the previous ones, although always involving memory, concerns information about the world. Dr. Cameron J. Camp identified and associated this difficulty with the phrase "on the tip of the tongue." This phrase makes it clear what the person may be feeling when they are trying to remember something from their life or past. It is a process that is very difficult for them because they know they know the name of the event but cannot remember it. This generates a lot of frustration, sadness, and anger.

Most people associate Alzheimer's disease and other forms of dementia (often senile) with memory loss. In fact, this is not the only thing that happens, and sometimes, not even the most important. There are three memory problems associated with dementia: the first involves learning new information and, the other two, involve remembering information already learned.

What Are the Damaged Memories?

- **Episodic memory:** the ability to remember personal episodes in one's life. As dementia progresses, one may forget things that happened the day before, the week before, and then the year before.
- **Semantic memory:** it concerns information about the world (vocabulary, the name of a grandchild, the capital of Belgium, etc). This information was learned in the past and stored in the memory, but it is not easy to retrieve it without help!

Let's take a look at the different ways in which caregivers\ families can put Montessori into practice:

- Older people can find comfort in holding dolls. A set of dolls and doll clothes can create an enjoyable activity.
- For those who like to bake or cook, baking ingredients in a safe cooking environment.
- Have a basket of clean socks that need to be matched and folded.
- Have a basket of clean towels to fold.
- Prepare tables with materials for activities such as puzzles, sorting exercises, and other games.
- Put out a container of plastic plumbing pipes that can be connected and assembled.

Dementia can cause difficulty controlling one's emotions or trouble with finding words. It can present as personality changes or an inability to focus or pay attention. Struggles with reasoning, thinking straight or remembering things are hallmarks of dementia.

The loss of cognitive functioning results in unusual behaviors. When we see these behaviors, there's trouble in the person's thinking, remembering, and/or reasoning. A problem in these functions means the disease is affecting the brain. This process is a part of brain failure. Brain failure is a term we don't often hear when talking about dementia, but it is what we're facing. Everyone has heard of heart failure. Most have heard of kidney failure. When these conditions of body systems cause an organ to not do its job properly, failure is the term used because the organ is now failing in its function in the body.

The same thing can happen to the brain. Dementia is a result of brain failure. When the heart fails, it can't properly pump blood to all parts of the body. When kidneys fail, they can't filter out toxins and excess fluid as blood passes through them. When the brain fails, it can't think straight, remember, or reason. A person with dementia is experiencing brain failure.

When It's Not Dementia

Delirium is another symptom sometimes confused with dementia. Unlike dementia, delirium comes on rapidly. An acute medical problem, like infection, brain injury, or metabolic imbalance, can cause delirium. Surgery can also lead to the sudden onset of delirium. Delirium may become permanent if untreated, so be sure to seek medical advice if your loved one has a rapid, marked decline in cognitive function.

An acute medical problem is one that occurs within a short period. People rarely decline overnight from dementia. An infection (such as a urinary tract infection, which we'll talk about later) is a much more likely culprit. Delirium comes on fast; dementia develops gradually.

Delirium manifests as severe confusion and rapid changes in functional abilities. Hallucinations or hyperactivity are often present. I often see delirium in older people during hospital stays. A person sick enough to need hospital care is sick enough to experience delirium.

The good news about delirium is that it generally goes away as the acute illness is treated. Delirium is not dementia. But a person with dementia is likely to experience delirium with any acute illness. We should think of delirium when someone with dementia has a sudden decline in function.

Symptoms of Alzheimer Disease

Anger and Aggression

Anger and aggression are the responses that strike fear in the hearts of dementia in seniors. Only about a third of people with dementia develop aggression. For those who do, it's the most common reason families are forced to place a loved one in a care facility.

Aggression is the verbal or physical result of anger gone unchecked. Humans get angry. Anger arises in response to perceived threats and unmet desires or expectations, or to hide emotions. When our brains are on track, the frontal lobe regulates our emotions, preventing wide swings to one extreme or another. The frontal lobe works to keep us on an even keel.

The frontal lobe also inhibits impulsive actions. Throat-punching your boss or taking your pants off in an overheated restaurant seldom ends well. The frontal lobe tells us, "Don't do that." Personality forms in the frontal lobe. Our level of tolerance for changing plans or unexpected outcomes is a part of our personality. We all know people who are easygoing. That trait is influenced by the frontal lobe.

When brain disease damages the frontal lobe, each of these functions falters. Anger easily slips into extremes of rage. No voice whispers, "Don't tell that lady she is fat." And any disruption of routine can cause profound distress. Brain failure of this kind leads to what professionals call "catastrophic reactions," another way to say "losing it" in 21 letters. Either way, you know it when you see it.

Aggression may be verbal and can feel just as devastating as physical violence. Seniors may be subject to all manner of verbal abuse. The saying that we always hurt the ones we love rings true in many households where dementia lives.

Violence, such as hitting, scratching or biting, may erupt from the smallest stressor. Try telling an adult with dementia that they can no longer drive or have access to knives for cooking. These necessary precautions can lead to a firestorm.

Anger and aggression are no laughing matter for dementia in seniors. The safety of both senior and care recipient may eventually require a professional care setting. Promises to never place a loved one in a home don't count when you're afraid to close your eyes at night.

There are things that we can do to reduce catastrophic reactions in our loved ones. Maintaining consistent routines, discovering triggers for aggression, and avoiding stressors can help. If your loved one has begun to display aggression, play detective. Learn what increases their stress level so you can step lightly around those triggers.

There are medications to reduce the frequency or severity of aggressive episodes. A practitioner may recommend antianxiety medications or prescribe a class of drugs called antipsychotics.

Antipsychotic drugs are controversial because of their potential side effects. On average, people taking antipsychotic drugs have a higher death rate than those who don't take them. A much more common side effect is oversedation. These drugs may affect balance, and falls may result.

The key is vigilance when using any medication that acts on the brain. The brain's response to a drug is extremely individualized. You can give 10 people the same drug at the same dose and get 10 different reactions. Finding the right drug for the right person is often a process of trial and error.

Most horror stories about medications come from putting people on a drug without monitoring their response. In some care facilities, the goal is to keep people quiet. Oversedation is the result. As long as you're watchful for this side effect, using antipsychotic drugs may be a good option.

Geriatric psychiatrists tend to be the most skilled in prescribing medications for aggression. Neurologists who are knowledgeable in this area seem to be rare. If my loved one was showing difficult behaviors or moods, I'd hotfoot to a geriatric psychiatrist.

Depression

"If you had dementia, you'd be depressed, too." I couldn't argue with the 66-year-old man sitting across from me. If you think the possibility of depression in someone with dementia means doctors routinely screen for it, think again. Underdiagnosis is rampant.

Diagnosing depression in someone with dementia is complicated because the two illnesses share so many symptoms. Many of the symptoms of depression mimic symptoms of dementia. It becomes a puzzle of which came first.

There are some important differences between depression and dementia. Depression onset takes place over weeks to a few months rather than the years of dementia onset. People in the early stages of dementia may feel ashamed, hopeless, or worthless following their diagnosis. These feelings are depression talking, not dementia.

Irritability, tearfulness, and appetite changes are common in depression. Social withdrawal and recurring thoughts of death or suicide are associated with depression. These symptoms are often more severe when due to depression than they would be with dementia alone.

I encourage you to request regular depression screenings for your loved one. If you notice signs or changes that may be depression, speak up. Ask that they be screened and treated if a diagnosis is confirmed. Treatment can help. You know your loved one; if you're concerned, you're probably right.

Treatment for depression may be medication-based or not. The best results come from a combination of approaches. This scenario is another one where a geriatric psychiatrist is best equipped to recommend treatment. As with all medication use, there should be close monitoring for usefulness and side effects.

Here's a tip to help both depression and anxiety: If you can find mindfulness-based stress reduction (MBSR) training near you or online, take it. If your loved one is in the early stages of dementia, take them along with you. There's strong evidence that MBSR can benefit both the senior and care recipient for years. With MBSR, seniors' burden declines and the need for facility care can be delayed. Difficult behaviors are less frequent and severe. These benefits continue long after the one with dementia has forgotten the training. It's worth an online search.

Memory Loss and Confusion

Memory loss is the symptom most people associate with dementia. Confusion in someone with dementia refers to being disoriented to time, place, or identity. The brain holds our memories, tells us who and where we are and allows us to discern time. As brain disease progresses, these functions begin to falter and eventually fail completely.

In the early stages of dementia, memory loss and confusion tend to be mild. In some ways, this phase is the most painful leg of the journey. Our loved one has lost enough brain cells to be confused and forgetful. But they still have the brainpower to know they don't know some things.

As brain failure progresses, confusion and memory loss grow. If a loved one says they've done the dishes for you, check the freezer. You wouldn't be the first to find dirty dishes "washed and put away" there. Correcting your loved one does nothing but upset and confuse them more. It's often hard to fathom how profound their confusion can be. We want to explain. We want to convince. We might as well want to hit the lottery. The odds of success are about the same.

One of the confusion's annoying traits is that it's seldom the same day to day. Has your loved one ever acted normally when company comes? Or kept it together for the five-minute phone call with your sibling, just long enough to convince said sibling that mom is fine and you're neurotic? It happens. Social graces can make it easy for people with dementia to fool us about how troubled they are. After holding themselves together for a while, our loved ones will likely be exhausted and more confused than ever. Shopping, social occasions, and health appointments are draining. It can take days to fully recover from what used to be so easy.

Although confusion can vary day to day, a sudden increase can be a sign of trouble. Dementia almost never progresses from one level to the next overnight. Changes over a few days are usually due to some acute problem in the body. The most common culprit is a urinary tract infection. Increased confusion due to infections or other acute illnesses is called delirium. It's important for physicians to recognize delirium rather than assume confusion is due to the patient's dementia. An accurate diagnosis will hinge on your input about your loved one's baseline before the acute illness.

The most common medications given in AD are to slow memory loss. Donepezil (Aricept) and memantine (Namenda) have been shown to delay decline on average; that is, in large groups, those taking these drugs declined more slowly than those not taking them. This average result does not predict individual responses to these meds.

Repetitive Actions

Few behaviors can pluck at a senior's nerves more than repetitive actions. When you've answered the same question eight times in the past half hour, it's hard to hear it again. Knowing that your loved one can't help it doesn't always make it easier. Observing repetitive actions is another occasion to put on your detective hat. The goal is to guess what feelings may be behind the action. Anxiety, loneliness, and boredom are common triggers.

People with dementia may worry about what they're supposed to be doing. Or they may be hungry, thirsty, in pain, or in need of a bathroom visit. When language fails, repetitive behaviors may be the only signal you get.

Constantly following you around often means your loved one needs to see you to know you're there. Drumming fingers or pacing can signal boredom or excess energy. A stressful environment or overstimulation can cause repetitive behaviors. Memory loss also comes into play here. Your loved one may not remember that they've already asked a question or that they just finished eating, so it's not time to fix another meal.

It's easy to tell you to just be patient. This reaction usually comes from someone who's not in the line of fire. You may be able to decrease repetitive behaviors, but eliminating them is hard. This situation is a prime example of why seniors must have time away on a regular basis.

Sundowning

Sundowning is an experience of increased confusion and agitation late in the day. It starts in the late afternoon and can last well into the night. Anxiety and aggression can develop. Some people hallucinate, seeing or hearing things that aren't there. There are multiple theories on what causes sundowning. A combination of factors makes the most sense. Dimming light and more shadows cause anxiety. They can also cause paranoia.

Fatigue is often a factor in both the person with dementia and the senior. By late in the day, both of you may have exhausted your energy stores. Fatigue shows in our face, tone of voice, and posture. Your loved one's anxiety and confusion may increase in response to your fatigue.

The brain regulates sleep-wake cycles. When the brain fails, a person's internal clock can go haywire. They may have trouble knowing whether it's night or day. Medications can also affect the sleep-wake cycle. A light sleeper with dementia may wake and believe their dream was reality. They may continue to act out their dream, which can lead to wandering or trying to leave the house. (See more on wandering.)

Sundowning can trigger placement in a care facility if left unchecked. Long-term sleep deprivation is used to torture prisoners of war. It effectively lowers the person's resistance to pressure. This result is no surprise to seniors who can't remember the last time they got a full night's sleep.

Wandering

Wandering or getting lost is common in people with dementia. In AD, getting lost in a familiar place can be one of the first signs of illness. There are lots of reasons someone might wander. It helps to look for reasons your loved one might be wandering. Stress and confusion in an unfamiliar place are one. Others are boredom, basic needs, like looking for the bathroom, or searching for someone or somewhere, such as a home.

Something to remember is that when people with dementia want to go "home," it's often their seniorhood home they are thinking of. Wandering can result from following old routines. If mom met the home bus at the corner every day for 65 years, she may head out now. Dad may be looking for the hardware store so he can fix those loose shingles. Never mind that it's 4:00 a.m.

Maintaining the safety of the wanderer is the top priority. Losing track of a loved one is every senior's worst nightmare. Given that two-thirds of those with dementia will wander, it's right to be concerned. The potential for a crisis is always there. Someone with dementia may not realize they're lost. They may not ask anyone for help. Or they may not remember their address or even their name. Most communities now have safe return programs operated through law enforcement or the Alzheimer's Association.

Memory Tips

Let's now look at some ways you can beef up your memory. In addition to the ability to acquire foreign languages, your brain has a high capacity to remember things at an amazing capacity and speed. Here are some tips that will help you get into the right place.

Stay Hydrated

One of the most important things we can do for our memories is to drink enough water. This point cannot be stressed enough. You need to drink plenty of fluids throughout your day. Otherwise, you will get dehydrated. Most of the body is filled with water, so we must find ways to hydrate ourselves throughout the day. Otherwise, we won't be as sharp as we want to be. Drink at least 2 to 3 liters of water per day. Your body and mind will feel the difference.

Drink Coffee or Tea: Caffeine Works Wonders

Many people drink caffeine to get their day started. It has proven benefits and can help us to be more energetic. In fact, drinking more coffee can help our digestive system and increase our memory because we can activate those neurons in our brains responsible for memory consolidation. In case you feel guilty about your addiction to caffeine or coffee, never fear. It will be helpful to your overall feeling and help you remember things a lot better. Not to mention, a jolt of caffeine every day will help you to concentrate on your important tasks. So, get you a cup of hot Americano from "Starbies." You will feel the difference in mind and body.

Try to Teach Someone Else What You Have Learned

It is no secret that the way to remember something is to teach others how to do it. You need to be able to explain in your own words a concept or idea. When you do this, your memory recall will be faster and more efficient. Find ways you can recycle your ideas. Hash it out with your friend and do a workshop on it. You will have a faster recall, and it will help you to master the content.

Think While You Walk and Talk

One efficient way to learn something effectively is by multitasking and doing something else while you're trying to master something. For example, when you walk and talk, you can effectively externalize your thoughts and also activate your memory, which takes in these experiences. It helps you to remember things much better. If you want to talk it out, you have to talk the walk. It is effective.

Study in a Stimulating and Low-Key Environment

When you are studying for a test or something else, find an environment that suits you. Whether that is in a library, at home in your living room, or at a coffee shop, find something that floats your boat. Often, it is in the low-key and stimulating environments where we can find our sweet spot for studying. Know what's right for you and do it. This will greatly help your concentration power and give you the skill needed to ace the tests you might have or remember things faster.

Play Instrumental Music While You Work or Study

Another method that may help your concentration and boost your memory power is playing low-key instrumental music no faster than 60 beats per minute. When you listen to music that has a lot of lyrics or instruments, it might distract you rather than help you. Find some study or concentration music on YouTube. There are plenty of choices, and you won't be disappointed. Find music that is meaningful to you and make it into your work or study jam. You will be able to be more effective in your memorization game.

Relax

Finally, you should find ways to relax because we often don't remember things well when we are tense or stressed. Find ways to live your life in a balanced and low-key way. Stay away from too much tension. Allow your stress to melt away. Relax, because life is short. And if you want to remember more effectively and faster, you should find ways to take a load off. Do it today, for your memory's sake.

The Best Foods to Help Prevent Alzheimer's Disease and Dementia in Seniors

The risk of Alzheimer's disease has never been greater than now. Due to lifestyles that have not been helpful, many people are faced with the possibility that they will lose their memories later in life. Not to fear, though. You can enhance your memory by eating the right foods. It has been shown that food is an essential part of developing your memory, and you should follow a healthy diet.

The key to preventing dementia is to eat a certain amount of the recommended foods as often as you can. You should not overeat red meat, processed foods, or bakery goods. Here are foods that are sure to help you in the process of preventing memory loss (Rosenbloom, 2018).

Dairy

Dairy products have many proven health benefits because they have lactic acid bacteria and fatty acids, which are produced during fermentation. Recent studies have noted the effects that these fermented dairy products can have on a person's ability to function cognitively. In short, foods like fermented cheese and yogurt can help a person prevent Alzheimer's disease and dementia.

Raw Leafy Greens

Greens, including spinach, kale, and romaine contain antioxidants and vitamin K. You should try to consume one cup of them every day.

Cruciferous Vegetables

Vegetables like broccoli, cauliflower, and Brussels sprouts contain a high quantity of vitamin K and glycosylates, which have antioxidants. To have the full effect, include three ½ cup servings in your meals during the week.

Blueberries

Many berries are helpful to the brain's function, and blueberries seem to have the most positive effects. They have flavonoids, which help the brain's pathways and mitigate the effects of aging. To improve your memory, eat ½ cup of any type of berries at least three times per week.

Beans

Currently, studies have been inconclusive as to why beans can be good for brain health, but it is possible that it is due to the number of antioxidants, fiber, and vitamins in them. To help you experience the effects, eat them instead of consuming red meat twice per week.

Nuts

Unsalted nuts contain a high content of antioxidants. Walnuts have a lot of omega-3 fatty acid, which helps the brain. Try to eat ¼ cup of nuts each day.

Fish

All types of fish contain iodine and iron, which foster steady cognitive function. Fish, like salmon and trout, have omega-3 fatty acids, which boost brain activity. Eat them once per week.

Whole Grains

Add oats, brown rice, and whole-grain wheat bread to your diet, which will also help you to have a healthier diet.

Chicken

Chicken is a good substitute for processed meat, but you should only take in one serving a day.

Olive Oil

For cooking, stick to olive oil as your main oil. Add it to your salad dressing. It has monounsaturated fats, vitamin E, and antioxidants.

Coffee and Caffeine

Caffeine in coffee has been associated with boosts in brain function and prevents a person from experiencing a cognitive decline from dementia. In addition, caffeine has been shown to improve memory, spatial memory, and working memory, which helps you experience a richer and healthier life.

Mediterranean Diet

In general, the Mediterranean diet has been shown to improve a person's ability to prevent themselves from getting dementia or cognitive decline. Therefore, it can significantly help a person to improve their overall health.

It is important to have a healthy lifestyle in addition to a healthy diet. Avoiding smoking and excessive drinking can help a person get on the right track. Risk factors for developing Alzheimer's disease include diabetes, high blood pressure, and obesity.

A Brain-Enhancing and Memory Improvement Menu

If you are looking to improve your cognitive function and have felt a bit foggy recently, then you may want to add brain-healthy foods to your diet. To help, let's look at the following one-day meal plan (*Power Up: One Day Brain Boosting Meal Plan*).

Food is medicine. If you want to gain energy and momentum, you should choose foods that are high in protein, vitamins, and minerals. When you are feeding your mind with good foods, make sure to add antioxidants, omega-3s, and vitamins because these will enhance your memory, lower your blood pressure, and help you to sharpen your mental skills.

Breakfast: Bowl of Oatmeal or Whole Grain Cereal with Berries

Breakfast has often been considered the most important meal of our day. It begins your metabolism, improves your mood, and helps with cognitive function. Oatmeal or whole-grain cereal is great for your brain and helps satiate your appetite for several hours. Carbs in the oats of oatmeal make glucose, which is your brain's primary fuel. Fiber will also help control your blood sugar and maintain a steady level.

To make this meal more interesting, you can add a variety of different toppings, such as blueberries, pomegranate seeds, Swiss cheese, brown sugar, and other things filled with nutrients.

Mid-Morning Snack: Blueberries

When you snack two to three times a day, you can regulate your metabolism and avoid getting hungry throughout the day. It also helps your blood sugar not to go down, which could decrease your brain's function. However, you should be careful to snack on the right kinds of foods, which include fruit, vegetables, nuts, and protein foods.

The right type of food that fits the bill is blueberries, which are filled with antioxidants and other nutrients that help your spatial memory. Put blueberries on your cereal, yogurt, or even create a smoothie for the results.

Lunch: Salad

Lunch is a critical moment for you to energize your brain. You should begin your lunch by taking some deep breaths to reduce stress and then enjoy a healthy salad that has lots of vegetables, shredded cheese, hard-boiled eggs, and nuts.

You should include some leafy greens that have a lot of vitamin K. Add cheese, which contains vitamin B12. You can add some vegetables with bright colors, such as green peppers, tomatoes, and broccoli, which have omega-3 fatty acids. Finally, pour on some olive oil or a balsamic vinaigrette to give your brain a good dose of monosaturated fats.

Afternoon Snack: Green Tea and Toast

One way you can prevent yourself from tanking in the middle of the afternoon is by adding some almond butter to a slice of toast. You can also have celery sticks and some hot green tea.

Nuts contain a high amount of vitamin E, which can help with cognitive function. Green tea contains the acid L-theanine, which promotes feel-good chemicals in the brain. The caffeine in the tea also helps with brain activity.

Dinner: Salmon with Lemon and Grilled Vegetables

Dinner is an important meal; you are wrapping up the day and you can enjoy time with friends or family, or spend your alone time with your favorite meal. One dish that is sure to please is salmon. It only requires 30 minutes to prepare, but it has memory-enhancing nutrients, including DHA and omega 3. If you add it to your diet twice a week, it can help reduce the risk of heart attack and stroke.

Dessert: Dark Chocolate

Everyone has some form of a sweet tooth, which means that dessert can be an indispensable part of our diet. After dinner, we can relish the sweet foods that bring us joy and boost our mood. Why not try some dark chocolate after your meal? You can add it to a glass of warm milk and enjoy the antioxidants that help improve your alertness and make you feel better. When you eat dark chocolate, you will feel good afterward, but you should be careful not to overdo it. Eat in moderation!

Mind Hacks Exercises for a Better and Happier Life

If you have successfully read this book to this point, congratulations to you, friend. That is the first step to achieving a successful mind hack.

The mind is another world, entirely, and to successfully hack the mind, you need some exercises and formulas to do so. After several thorough research, I have come up with different mind games/hackings/exercises that will help you create the life you desire.

Squirrel

One habit which often deprives us of a happy and desirable life is multitasking. Multitasking is a natural tendency of man. Most humans, which 70% includes you, have the tendency to multitask. It is quite addictive, and addictive things give us pleasure. There is a wealth of scientific research that shows that multitasking means "doing several things badly at once." As you wait in line at a restaurant, do you tend to pull out your phone? As you are preparing to get the night's sleep, do you check your WhatsApp messages? This is one of the addictive natures that damages one's well. It is due to the vagueness and manipulation of the mind. Often, we carry out this habit incessantly that the mind perceives it as normal.

To stop this addiction, one mind game is needed to be carried out. Try to become more aware of feeling being "broken away" from your present activity. Keep a track of how many interruptions you notice. At the end of the day, write down the final number on your practice pad.

The One Hour Investment

Another way of reprogramming your thinking is to carry out the "one-hour investment."

Distractions!! Distractions!!! Distractions!!!! We all face them every now and then. Let's face it, we all face distractions no matter how little. These distractions, no matter their magnitude, have a ripple effect in affecting us from attaining our goals. The reason why you have not accomplished those New Year resolutions you set earlier this year, the reason why you are lagging in your career is not because of your background or whatever excuse you give, it is mostly because of distractions!!

Do not fall into the trap of wasting the whole day in a bid to reclaim your time. It doesn't work that way. It's all about simplification. Be simple in your attempt to carry out this mind hack. Spend one hour turning off unnecessary distractions such as text messages, Instagram newsfeed notifications, and unnecessary emails inter alia.

Also, set a recurring appointment in your calendar to eliminate further. Count the number of distractions you turned off and record the numbers in your private pad. This will eventually reprogram your mind into eliminating distractions by itself. You can also retrain your mind by carrying out meditation or mindfulness.

Hack Through Imagination

Imagination is another vital mind hack exercise. It is an obvious fact that nothing can be achieved until you see it in your mind. There is a secret treasure in your mind that you can successfully hack to accomplish great things. Imagination is a hard mental work. Out of the mental hacks, it is probably the hardest. From experience, it is as hard as actual physical work. Through mind hacking, you learn the "feel" of imagining. You don't shy away from it. Instead, you constantly engage in it. Only through exercising, this active visualizing component can build up its power and strength.

"Imagination, then realization." Now, inhale and exhale gently, close your eyes, imagine: What is the one thing you would like to have? Do not rush the process, do it gently, write down what you imagine on your practice pad.

Write Now

Another way to mind hack is to actually write things down. After concentration, writing is the next big thing. There is a great power that comes from writing things down. It gives us the capability to actually have the willpower to accomplish what we desire. Your mind hacking skills will be greatly enhanced by simply writing things after the concentration game. And I trust you've started practicing the concentration game. The idea here is to spend twenty minutes in concentration, then utilize a few minutes to write your positive loops. Its total time commitment is less than half an hour.

Writing down is a powerful mind exercise as it gives you the chance to actually reflect. Writing down, you may find valuable ideas come to you. Simply think of this exercise as your internal Thomas Edison laboratory. There is incredible and mind-altering power in repetition. How do you go about this exercise? After completing your concentration game, write down each of your positive loops on your practice sheet.

Share the Dream

It may sound like a surprise, but sharing your dream with others is another way to enhance your mind hacking skills. Collaborating with other people helps you a lot in achieving your dreams. Ideas are a funny thing. They are usually accomplished when shared with like minds.

"When ideas are shared, the possibilities do not add up, they multiply"- Paul Roomer. Sharing your ideas make them better. By collaborating, we give our ideas new ways to connect. Mind hacking is an open source because we want it to be collaborative. How do you go about this exercise? Share one of your positive loops with one of your confidantes. Be brave when doing so! Write down the person's name on the practice sheet at the end of the book. N.B. does not collaborate unenthusiastically; strives for a radical kind of collaboration. Swallow that arrogance of yours and get yourself out there. Stretch your prospect!

Focus Your Mind Like a Laser

Another mind exercise is to focus your mind like a laser. You see, your mind is like a laser. To begin with, a laser is a focused light. A laser takes a light and focuses it into a high-powered beam that can destroy missiles from space. In correspondence, the energy of our mind is so numerous that it diffuses over different thoughts. However, with mind hacking, we can focus this mental energy just like a laser on a particular thought. This focused mental energy enables us to accomplish tiny goals that move us towards those "big" goals of ours. The term LASER can also serve as an acronym for a good sub-goal.

A sub-goal should be:

- Limited
- Achievable
- Specific
- Evaluated
- Repeatable

An easy way to get started with any of these tiny goals is simply to ask the question, "What is the next step?" After asking yourself this, spend sixty seconds in stimulation on this one goal. Later on, write and check off each sub-goal on your practice sheet.

The final mind hack is to ask, "Who am I?" You are different from your mind. You are a different entity entirely. Thus, the question is the ultimate mental hack and loop. This is the stage where we enter the philosophical and mystical realm. Finding the 'you' behind the "You" is the ultimate mystery. It is the ultimate frontier to hacking the mind. Everything since the beginning of the book has been revolving around what is behind the working of the mind, which is "you." It is when you find out this answer that you can begin living that fulfilling life.

Managing Stress and Anxiety

Do not forget that stress activates a flight or fight response, a reaction that births all other outcomes. To be on the safer side, it is essential that you equip yourself with the tips that could help you manage stress positively and use it to your advantage. The following would help you manage stress positively.

- Identify stress triggers and avoid or replace them.
- Keep a positive mindset always.
- Eat healthy meals and exercise regularly.
- Do what you want and when you want.
- Do things one step at a time.
- Rest and sleep.
- Plan your schedule and manage your time effectively.
- Find time to relax your body and mind—for instance, meditation and yoga.

How to Deal with Anxiety

To deal with anxiety, the general idea is to get relaxed and stay in touch with reality. It is a psychological process that has you trying to take back mental control in times of anxiety. You can try the following:

- Intentionally redirect your mind.
- Identify your anxiety triggers.
- Manage your worries. For instance, set time to period, know them, and solve them.
- Rest and exercise.
- Avoid overthinking and overgeneralization.

- Learn to live in the present.
- Practice self-love and care.
- Meditation and positive affirmations.
- Try group or medical support.

Stress and anxiety are powerful emotions that can overload your mind and make it unnecessarily hard to enjoy the benefits of mind hacking. Their effects are both physical and mental. Because they seem to have positive and negative sides, there is still a chance that you could use them positively. However, you must understand them, their nature, triggers, and symptoms as an essential part of managing them effectively. I believe this chapter has exhaustively discussed that. Henceforth, it is very important that you should be ready for them. What makes this a needed commitment is the fact that these emotions could be triggered at any point in time. So, in order to manage these emotions effectively, you must stay in control at all times.

How Seniors Can Live a Happy Life

There's an unfortunate reason why happiness is typically elusive—our minds simply aren't wired to do this. Instead, our minds have progressed to endure, to safeguard ourselves, to keep us risk-free. Certainly, we have minutes of elation as well as periods of contentment and happiness. Numerous of us are tormented with consistent unfavorable feelings—we are simply ordinary stuck in the "blahs."

Exactly, how do we find much more pleasure in our life? Like anything else, it takes practice to grow recurring happiness. In a sense, we have to reset our baseline. It will not happen overnight; however, below are the top 20 things you can do daily to discover the tricks of being better.

1. Concentrate on the Positive

To find lasting joy, you require to retrain your mind from a negative way of thinking to a favorable state of mind. Try something like spending 1 to 2 minutes searching for positives in your life. Do this 3 times a day for 45 days, as well as your brain will certainly begin doing it automatically.

Choose a positive concept for the day—something you will repeat to yourself, such as "Today is gorgeous" or "I really feel grateful for all I have." Also, when points go south, take a minute to try as well to see it from a positive light. Never underestimate the value of identifying the silver linings in life.

2. Celebrate Little Triumphs

Life has plenty of ups and also downs, but in between, we have a lot of little success that goes unnoticed. Take a minute to celebrate these small successes. Did you mark off all the important things on your order of business that you've been procrastinating on? Yay! Did you ultimately clear out a thousand e-mails that have been filling your inbox? Woohoo! Get a kick out of these little achievements. They build up!

3. Discover Your Work-Life Balance

Job occupies a great deal of our day; however, it should not be the only thing we do. It's important to seek tasks and also interests beyond our job. Do you have a pastime? Are you hanging out with friends as well as liked ones? Are you obtaining a workout? Producing balance in your life will certainly minimize stress and anxiety and give you various other outlets to express yourself and enjoy.

4. Practice Mindfulness

Mindfulness meditation works by bringing your understanding as well as focus to today's minute. It's concerning being nonjudgmental and accepting just how you are feeling. Exercising mindfulness implies existing, being conscious as well interested. Approving what we are going through reduces stress and anxiety as well as assists us see scenarios wherefore they are. Via mindfulness, we can discover peace as well as an affirmation in ourselves.

5. Be Imaginative

You may think about artists as being irritable and depressed, yet studies show that engaging in innovative tasks on a regular basis makes you happier. Those that hang around utilizing their creativity as well as being innovative have much more enthusiasm and also are most likely to have feelings of lasting joy as well as wellness. Such imaginative tasks can include creating, paint, drawing, and also music performance.

6. Approve Imperfection

Several of us strive for perfection—we desire to press ourselves to be our best. In order to be absolutely happy, you have to embrace the blemish part of life.

7. Do What You Enjoy

Don't waste the best years of your life on a joyless task, also if it's paying the costs. Focus on developing a career in an area that encourages you and also will certainly supply you with a high level of fulfillment, as well as your happiness element will certainly go up significantly.

8. Invest Carefully

Investing money in experiences (traveling, eating, shows, and so on) can make us better since we are sharing those experiences with others. Joy attached to product properties discolors, yet experiences assist us in defining our objective and also enthusiasm in life.

9. Stay in the Moment

Our thoughts and feelings usually focus on the past or the future. Truth is what you are experiencing in this actual minute; what you are experiencing today. Occasionally, we intend to escape that truth. However, when we stay in the present, we are totally engaged in our lives. Undertake to stay in the minute and you'll start to have a much deeper recognition for your life.

10. Grow Gratitude

Thankfulness is a glad admiration for what you have actually received in life. When you spend time each day acknowledging all that is great in life, you'll see there is even more excellence than you understand, and also, you'll locate that depression, sadness, and also stress, and anxiety are reduced.

11. Repay

Be charitable with your time, as well as your cash. Those that are generous in investing money in others tend to have excellent health and wellness, possibly because offering has a feel-good impact that reduces blood stress as well as anxiety.

12. Surprise Yourself

It's hard to feel delighted if you are bored or feeling blah regarding life. Component of sensation delighted is feeling stimulated, interested, and a little stunned by life. Set goals on your own and also then function to accomplish them.

13. Listen to As Well As Engage with Music

Paying attention to songs raises our spirits. It makes us really feel better, partially because paying attention to songs causes our minds to release dopamine, a neurochemical connected to pleasure, and also reward. Those that engage with music via dance or through going to shows report high degrees of joy and a sense of health.

14. You Do You

One of the best things you can do to boost your happiness is to just be on your own. Spend some time getting to know on your own. Look for methods to be comfy in your own skin.

15. Build Significant Relationships

Happiness, relationships, neighborhood, and love go hand in hand. As people, we have a basic need to link and also engage with others. We naturally seek our people, those who will support us, comprehend us, and be there for us through life's rollercoaster flight. Without meaningful relationships, we are lonely as well as separated. When we pursue happiness with others, we're better.

16. Absolutely Nothing Contrasts with You

Social media has a method of making us feel like everyone else has it better than us. Enabling envy and also bitterness to take origin burglarizes us of valuing what we have.

17. Stop Worrying

Worries torment your mind as well as make you concerned and also afraid about points you commonly have no control over. Occasionally, we believe that if we fret sufficiently, we can keep negative points from happening.

18. Hang Out with Happy Individuals

It transforms out that sensations can be moved from

one individual to another, and the more we share experiences with one another, the much more our habits and also feelings end up being synchronized. One secret to lasting joy is surrounding yourself with others who are also happy.

19. Hang Out in Nature

Some scientists think that today's ultra-wired generation is struggling with a nature-deficit problem. Research has shown that the even more time we spend in nature, and the more we relate to the environment around us, the better our sense of joy. Our connection to nature likewise plays a role in keeping favorable psychological health.

20. Recollect Over Pleased Memories

Maybe, since fond memories make us delighted, when we remember great times and delighted memories, we can raise our positive self-image and feel closer to those around us.

CONCLUSION

Thank you for making it through to the end of this Montessori seniors book. The most interesting part is that however much the adults feel responsible and take credit for their seniors' growth, learning, and development. Seniors happen to learn at their own pace, and while doing so, they only need facilitation in the form of a properly set environment, positive attitude of adults, and guided freedom to learn and explore. This alone can make a remarkable difference in their personality as they shape it according to the opportunities given to them.

Properly implemented, Montessori Method and scientific approach can be highly effective in producing men capable of not only reasoning and solving problems, but independently efficient in their work and deriving pleasure from it. This sort of mindset after being raised as a Montessori senior shows that education is not just for task completion for vocational induction, but it is for life and is life itself. The Montessori seniors are socially confident, emotionally stable human beings with spiritual love and a sense of responsibility present at their very core.

Made in United States
North Haven, CT
04 October 2023

42346669R00078